LOVE RISE

LOVE RISE UP

an anthology

POEMS OF SOCIAL JUSTICE, PROTEST & HOPE

edited by

STEVE FELLNER & PHIL E. YOUNG

with an introduction by **DALE DAVIS**

2012 · Benu Press, Hopkins MN

12 13 14 15 16   7 6 5 4 3 2 1   FIRST EDITION

Paperback edition and electronic edition

Printed in the United States

Design by Claudia Carlson, www.claudiagraphics.com

Text set in Minion and display in Helvetica Neue

ISBN: 978-0-9844629-6-4 (paperback)

Library of Congress Control Number: 2012938418

P.O. Box 5330
Hopkins, Minnesota 55343-9998
www.benupress.com

This book is dedicated to
Louise Young,
who honors the world
with her faith, hope, and perseverance.

PREFACE

I did something stupid and came to jail, and that's when I thought it was over. When I met Dale Davis, she told me I had a gift to offer the world. I started writing about the streets...my time in jail making it day by day. When I die, I don't want people crying. I want people saying his words stopped me from hurting someone else.

Words as an agent of power and change. These particular words were written by an incarcerated youth. They were relayed and spoken during the opening of "Freedom of Expression: An Exhibition of Contemporary Diaries," which took place at the Anne Frank Center in New York. Hopefully, testimonials such as these help make it clear why when we started this project we turned to Dale Davis to write the introduction for this book. Dale is one of the founding poets of New York State Poets in the Schools, a co-founder of The New York State Literary Center, and one of the founders of the Association of Teaching Artists. Her lifetime of work concentrates on education programs for young people at the highest risk of educational failure, in residential placement and day treatment facilities, juvenile detention centers, juvenile justice facilities, and jails. For someone as honorable as Dale Davis, her successes go hand in hand with tangible, world change.

Dale Davis is a true agent of social justice and progress. So are many of the poets in this book. In our current historical moment, cynicism and despair are perhaps as widespread as they've ever been. For the purposes of this anthology, we readily acknowledge that reality, but hopefully push back against it, wishing to reassert the comfort, strength, and inspiration literature can offer to communities and social movements. We wanted a book that others could carry (and that we could carry ourselves), that defied cynical times and, as a collected piece, offered a portrait of the power of struggle and the potentiality of true change. In artistic imagination, possibility resides and comes into being. Ideally, this collection will generate thoughts of both "look at what's been overcome" and "look at what we need—and can—still do." For this collection, we chose poets who offered us two things that naysayers say can't exist: the complete merging of politics and beauty.

Allison Joseph's "Xenophilia" perhaps best demonstrates the idea that language by its very nature is a most political act:

Whisper secrets only your people know,

untranslatable lullabies lilting me into sleep
deeper than rivers by towns now wiped
off any map, a disappeared cartography.

Just as Gabriela Erandi Rico puts forth the call to:

Endure,
Resist
Stand and Reclaim!

The divine intersection of music and protest bursts through Jillian Weise's "Dear Poets, Stop Using the Disabled as Tragic Figures in Your Poems." It begins with a collective voice declaring: "We all met & we agreed..../We know you're just using us to affect pity & grief, pity & grief, a dash of poverty." It ends with reassurance and demand: "Please don't be mad at me very much. I too believe in beauty."

That strange and surprising relation between art and politics appears in the most private and public of realms. We deliberately attempted to include some poems that might not, at first, appear to be overtly concerned with social justice, but arrive in the same neighborhood in unexpected and subtle ways. Consider these lines from Rodney Jones' "Doing Laundry," with his masterful understanding of how an ostensibly simple domestic act becomes something charged with social power and equality:

I who popped rivets into the roof of a hangar,
Who herded copper tubes into the furnace,
Who sweated bales of alfalfa into the rafters...

When I tied steel on the bridge, I was not so holy
As now, taking the hot sheets from the dryer,
Thinking of the song I will make in praise of women
But also of ordinary men, doing laundry.

Many of these poems are explicit reminders of real events, true injustice, and begin to suggest the opposing forces that rise out of such moments. Colette Inez's poem "Miss Sealy," for example, literally places us at a threshold, a doorway that marks the kind of seemingly immovable objects the Civil Rights movement would overcome. Eliot Khalil Wilson's stirring "Several-Hundred Mile Fence" focuses on a more recent real-life tragic incident that involved a twenty year old migrant worker. Here are the closing lines of the poem:

Call them a gang, call them all criminals
but no fence or gunship or law or razor wire
will stop their belonging. They belong.
See them like a boundless, shattered stained-glass window,

like hinges to unlockable doors.

We could have chosen any number of poets to illustrate our points. Diversity was crucial. Not only did we make cultural and aesthetic difference an imperative, but we made an effort to have brand new poets standing next to the veterans. We choose not to follow a traditional, chronological approach but instead wanted the poems to play off one another in sometimes unexpected ways. We believe there is no such thing as the best. Instead, there are shifting collectives trying to be of service to something beyond themselves, as in the case of these poets' work. We admire each of them for showing us the way literature can actually make something happen.

Steve Fellner & Phil E. Young
March 21, 2012

INTRODUCTION

Love Rise Up confronts the reality of social justice. We all are entitled to the same rights. Yet, too often, *the unspoken wondering / if any of us is safe* (from a line by Cheryl Dumesnil in "Hard Labor") can lead to silence, fear, or smoldering anger. Dumesnil writes of the "silver path." *Love Rise Up* is a path before us towards the dignity of all human beings.

Langston Hughes in "Daybreak In Alabama" writes, "When I get to be a composer / I'm gonna write me some music about / Daybreak in Alabama." Patrick Bizzaro, Christopher Hennessy, Anne Panning, and Gabriela Erandi Rico are composers. Theirs is the music of daybreak, poems that illuminate greater gender, racial, and ethnic equality.

The poems in *Love Rise Up* are narratives of social justice that not only define it but challenge us to meet it head-on. The poets invite us to touch it and to feel it. The poems are the language to quote Clay Matthews, "to make it all fit together."

They collectively leave us with important questions. How do we respond to those who have come before in the struggle for social justice? What do we add to their work and sacrifice? A line in Marvin Bell's "The Dead Have Nothing To Lose By Telling the Truth" reads "What can they do to gain our attention?" Bell's last line is "He feels the human cry in his bones." This gathering of poets is the human cry. "What is it that I've learned?" Sam Hamill asks. Or as Patricia Jabbeh Wesley proposes in "Ghosts Don't Go Away Just Like That:"

> They want to know if we will put up a stone or keep
>
> the fire burning to put out the fires, to stop all the killing
> in the city streets, around the world, to stop
>
> all the killings in the eyes of the city streets.

These questions become: what will I do with what I have learned? What will I do to put out the fires?

Dale Davis
January 17, 2012

CONTENTS

LOVE RISE UP

LANGSTON HUGHES

Daybreak in Alabama

When I get to be a composer
I'm gonna write me some music about
Daybreak in Alabama
And I'm gonna put the purtiest songs in it
Rising out of the ground like a swamp mist
And falling out of heaven like soft dew.
I 'm gonna put some tall tall trees in it
And the scent of pine needles
And the smell of red clay after rain
And long red necks
And poppy colored faces
And big brown arms
And the field daisy eyes
Of black and white black white black people
And I'm gonna put white hands
And black hands and brown and yellow hands
And red clay earth hands in it
Touching everybody with kind fingers
And touching each other natural as dew
In that dawn of music when I
Get to be a composer
And write about daybreak
In Alabama.

Indigenous Spirit (Of Essence & Presence)

to Chief Billy Tayac and his son, Mark

It's in the color
of our people
It's in the pain
within our soul
It's in the meaning
of our dances
It's in the drum-beat
of a call...

It's in the relevance
of history
It's in the feelin'
dispossessed
It's in the words
Indian Nation!
It's the resistance
in our heads

It's in the word
Assimilation
Colonization of our minds
It's in oppression and
injustice
Regression means
one step behind

It's in the
genocide of nations
Bleeding babies
Chopped off hands
500 years of
our castration
Survival means
taking a stand.

It's reservations
It's Aztlan
It's trans-frontera nacional
It's pan-American
liberation
Un movimiento
hasta el final!

It's in the brown
earth that we cherish
It's in the smoke
of our copal
It's in our prayers
to Creator
It is massacres
in Acteal

It's persecution
of the Mayas
Having to speak
these foreign tongues
It's the endurance
of the Yaqui
It's in our old
It's in our young

It's in the sad eyes
of my Tata
It's in the wrinkles
on his face
It's in our struggle
to continue
It is our history and fate

It's in the spirit
of our ancestors
We are Indigenous
Ain't it the same?
It's in the blood
that we have tasted
Endure,
Resist
Stand and Reclaim!

BRENT GOODMAN

"One Nation Under Me"

— GOD
(on a highway billboard)

Whose? The Cooper Mini cutting me off
asks my bumper to "Coexist." Stay in your own lane
my horn exclaims. Once when I was an infant my father
pressed a Manischewitz-soaked cloth to my tongue.
Generations circled me, the Rabbi
slowed his hand and breath. I was sculpted
to be defined by what is not a part of me.
There is a wall we love so much we kiss it.
Is this why I inherit barbed wire? Why
my grandmother suffered her first stroke shortly after
my uncle's shiksa wedding beneath a crucifix?
How easy it is to whistle across state lines
when the radio keeps singing an indistinct song.
At the truck stop cafe the TV is muted, though
dark teenagers throw stones through a cloud of teargas
and they remind you of thieves. My first sensation
was a scalpel. I'm driving to the capital
to learn what makes my history fathomless
or miraculous. Never forget this starkly-lit exhibit:
chest-high piles of black shoes, pocket watches,
gold teeth. God makes choices
and I am one of them. We ask our prophets
to write laws so we won't have to later. Every man
and his son shall cover his head before
your eyes. Grandma raised me to avert my stare
when anyone darker slunk by, which must be why
I thought only some of us could ever be seen.
God makes choices and sometimes we are not cruel.
Still I pray for safe parking. All day at the Holocaust Museum
fortunately I learn the final solution to the Jewish question
is another question, only kinder. God makes choices and so
do we, I tell the infant in my father's arms. Generations
enter my living room. The oldest tree in the yard
leans its shadow against the curtained window.

DAN BELLM

The weight

You must prepare to carry nothing
where you walk,

a God who cannot be seen,
a name you cannot speak — —

therefore gather
the most precious of what you have,

and build me something heavy you can carry,
heavy as you want.

I will be weightless in it,

an idea, a promise,
among you, within you —

I will be unbearable. You can bear it.

Over and over you will pick it up
and set it down,

and as you wander
you will lose what you brought forth,

the ark will collapse in your hands,
the stones of the law will break.

Then you will carry me in your minds,
in your mouths —

unbearable as you want. You can bear it.

Terumah, Exodus 25:1–27:19

CHERYL DUMESNIL

Hard Labor

for Teri

Six-o'clock alarm broke the morning open
and we choked down gas station coffee, drove
to the lake, watched familiar cars creep up
the gravel road, tired bodies carrying
hammers, a cooler, charcoal, a red gas can.
Then Teri fired up her neighbor's chainsaw
and we axed the storm-toppled maple to logs —
hours bagging damp brush, hauling branches
to the road, wood glue and box screws
to steady the weathered picnic table's legs.
Then, after a tour of the latest additions — sheetrock
walls for an upstairs bedroom, the cherry wood
banister she found in some old man's barn —
after scraping the grill, stacking briquettes, after
coaxing the fire and everyone complaining
Teri does things the hard way — this house
an hour out of town, built by small paychecks
and her own hands. After well-earned burgers
and all the laughing, we agree, we wouldn't
give this up for anything — aching muscles,
swamp mud caking our shoes, sawdust
ground into our palms, white corn steaming
in its foil. After hard talk around the table
about who's out and who's hiding, the young.
man beaten unconscious Friday night for
wearing pink, and the unspoken wondering
if anyone of us is safe, we sat in silence
on the dock edge, bare feet tapping rings
into the lake, and watched a harvest orange
moon rise through the trees, casting across
the water a silver path anyone would take.

JILLIAN WEISE

Dear Poets, Stop Using the Disabled as Tragic Figures in Your Poems

We all met & we agreed.
We've seen ourselves standing on the corners of your poems begging.
We've seen ourselves limping along the subway platforms of your poems crying.
We've seen ourselves blind in the metaphors, deaf in the similes, of your poems.
We've seen so many phantom limbs in your poems we wonder
if there's a Phantom Limb Repository. And who is The Clerk?
To whom shall we address our complaint?
We've smelled ourselves in your poems & we smell bad.
We know you're just using us to affect pity & grief, pity & grief, a dash of poverty.
We're no longer effective on those terms.
We're taking us back.
I'm taking a break.
I'm giving an oral exam to a grad student.
She talks about Byron & his 1,000 lovers.
She talks about *Don Juan*.
"*Don Juan* written by a man with a club foot," I say.
"What do you mean?" she says.
No one told her. No one ever tell anyone. Everyone be quiet.
Shhhhhhh! Don't say anything. Don't read *that* into it.
Dear Poets: I'm reading *that* into it. I'm saying.
Please don't be mad at me very much.
I too believe in beauty.

WILLIAM HEYEN

Emancipation Proclamation

Whereas it minds its own mind
& lives in its one place so faithfully
& its trunk supports us when we lean against it
& its branches remind us of how we think

Whereas it keeps no bank account but hoards carbon
& does not discriminate between starlings & robins
& provides free housing for insects & squirrels
& lifts its heartwood grave into the air

Whereas it holds our firmament in place
& writes underground gospel with its roots
& whispers us oxygen with its leaves
& so far survives our new climate of ultraviolet

Whereas it & its kind when we meet beneath them
shade our sorrows & temper our prayers
& their colors evoke our dream of beauty
from before we were born into this hereafter

We the people for ourselves & our children
necessarily proclaim this tree
free from commerce & belonging to itself
as long as it & we shall live.

CLAY MATTHEWS

Civil War

I've been teaching leads and introductions
in my composition class. That was a bad beginning
about beginnings, but I need to start somewhere,
and it's not always easy to know where, or why,
or what's best. Yesterday I was conferencing
with one of my students, Matthew, a Liberian
who was fortunate enough to escape the war
and come to America. Matthew had a heartbreaking
lead, he's writing about his experience in the war,
he started with a story about the rebels coming
to his home, how his family hid his small cousin
under a bed, then how the rebels dragged them all
out into the road, found his cousin, shot him
in front of them all, and then hurt his two sisters.
I didn't know what to say. This is good,
is what came out, but it wasn't good, it was wrong,
and my imagination failed to understand it.
I've talked to Matthew several times about transforming
his biographical experience into a research paper.
It's getting better every day. The paper is eventually
supposed to make a critique of the U.N., noting
how they came to Liberia to help in small numbers,
but once they were shot at by the rebels packed up
and went home. We all have lives, and it's difficult
sometimes to know where to stand up. I see celebrities
all the time arguing for this cause or that. I see politicians
saying something must be done. But it all seems so far away,
and somewhere along the road I've become cautious
about calling something right or wrong. But some things
are wrong no matter how many times you turn them
around in your hands. Killing a child. Hurting children.
We've all heard the stories before, but it's important
to me right now to keep telling them. At the end
of yesterday's meeting Matthew, which is part of my own
last name, which means gift of god, told me a friend
had suggested that he write all his experiences down,
that he put them into a book. He said it was something
he wanted to do, but that he still had problems
with the language, with how to make it all fit together.

I guess I need some help, he said, and I told him
I would be glad to, and wondered if he would take me
up on it. Then he left, walking out of the fluorescent light
of the classroom, and I thought about one story
passing into another, I thought about Afghanistan,
my own sisters, my wife, my life. Sometimes the answers
are easy, as simple as that sounds — like an ocean
crashing rhythmically against another shore.

MATTHEW HITTINGER

What Part of *Don't Ask, Don't Tell*
Don't You Understand?

Gettysburg, PA —
    families crowd the run-down visitor's
       center — school groups cloud
    dim glass around guns — the tour guide ponders
       my question confused
    perhaps at the thought of a she-poet
    buried but feet from the fallen soldiers
    perhaps at our interest in her — we
       do not know the names
          of his soldiers — he
    does not know the work
          of nor the name Ms.
             Marianne Moore —

so we put aside Ms.
    Moore decide the self-guided auto-tour
       will cure our boredom
    justify the drive — placards match numbers
       on the map plastic
    protecting a script I read silently
    you read out loud intent on how photo
    reproductions match, recreate landscape —
       it was not until
          our hike up Big Round
    Top — tulip trees full
       their fallen blossoms
          yellow-green, flower

circumscribed with orange —
    that I understood — two black butterflies
       circled encircled
    each wing each grave — O copse, highwater mark
       of a divided
    nation — O blue fishhook inside gray, side
    broke against side, the bodies flayed, corpses
    corpses — and now almost a century
       and a half later
          what hangs on those fields —

silence — silence — say
the word write silence
until it sounds looks

wrong — silence as deep
or deeper than the park's requested peace —
it could not can not
consecrate like the consecration made
those July days — no
cemetery designated private
or public holds the living's thoughts at bay —
take this soldier who weeps a man nursing
a man, man's last words
to another, two
men ambiguous
as daguerreotypes
that portray two men

no context or sign
of relationship, the action at hand —
here one man dies while
his comrade survives — features fade and merge
memory fails me
transforms memorial, idealizes
the texture of a beard the expression
exchanged eyes locked on the eyes of the one
who dies spark of life
lost no words no words —
lost like the failed points
of light as they flexed
across field and ridge

the Cyclorama
map's topography a palm's contours lost
like that blood-flecked tooth
I cradled at age seven crown and roots
nestled in my life
line's crease — I tasted iron as my tongue
tip touched socket, shot back like a palm bit
from a metal nip found beneath the pillow —
vigil — keep vigil
bronze soldier vigil
over your comrade
dying beneath you —
no retreat — no peace —

RANE ARROYO

In Praise Of Shirley Chisholm

My first vote for president went to you,
Ms. Chisholm; it was a time when we all
were poets: the jungle emeralds, the red

rivers of blood, the brown enemy and
the White Congress. There was your
face, your secret Barbados accent speaking

for us who spoke but never echoed by
laws. Homer and I knew Nixon would
make sure our bodies became puppets,

a modern slavery in sweaty uniforms far
from familial prayers. You knew you'd
lose your bid, but Quixote'd your way to

the spotlight. How could we do less in
our lives? We grew our Viking hair and
Afros; we made love as if our beds (and

floors) were embassies that could give us
political refuge. It's hard work to be safe,
to own the future that's ours to bewitch.

GLENN SHELDON

Years Unite to Become Centuries

There is much in accumulation:
snow becoming snowstorms,
books burning to reveal
libraries as our only eternities.

One poet murdered by a revolution
leads to other poets hanging naked
in another dictator's courtyard.

One kiss can become kisses,
all the prodigal sons returned home
at the same time: laughter unleashed.

Not one wine bottle to toast with
but millions.

Not a stampede by one, but by hundreds
of humans with purpose
(in a universe placing its bets on chaos).

A tree looks solid, until its rings
are revealed, ripples in a secret history.

Then there are the mass graves,
where names become one — The-Stolen-From-Us.

Never forget or become forgettable, for
zero is a trickster, a turncoat, a secret tyrant.
The calendar is both a powerful ally and a foe.

JUDY RAY

A Few Seconds of Modern History

Tiananmen Square, Beijing, 6/89

We never saw his face,
the lone man in shirtsleeves
who made his dance like a matador,
who declared his poem
in front of eighteen tanks
with iron tread of history
rolling through Beijing.

We never knew his name,
the lone man in shirtsleeves
who sidestepped neatly
to challenge the gun-sights
as the first tank swung a little
like an elephant shifting weight
from one leg to the other.

We never heard his voice,
the slim man who waved his arms,
clambered up on the tank to beg peace,
saying to the soldiers, "Look at us!
We are your brothers and sisters."
He stepped down, still protesting, led back
to join other offside citizens.

We never knew what happened
to the brave man on a June day
who danced his defiance across the Square,
heroic as Horatius, but unarmed.
What brilliance there must have shone
in his dark eyes to light for us
this stark scene of resistance.

MARVIN BELL

The Dead Have Nothing to Lose by Telling the Truth

On the Fiftieth Anniversary of the Adoption of
The Universal Declaration of Human Rights.

He sees the leaves fly free.
She sees the wild horse and the sparrow.
Free to labor, to consort with their kind, to choose or be chosen.
He sees them fed and feeding, mindful of the season.
She hears the continents shifting, he smells the air of change.
He tastes the wind-borne soot of rebirth.
She feels the human cry in her bones.

What can they do to gain our attention?
Shall he dance, shall he spin in the air, shall he vote with his feet, with his voice,
with the shells of his burning ears?
Shall she tell the world to hear the world's crying?
Shall she number the bodies, the prisons, the pyres, shall he mark the graves,
display the bloody shackles?
How many pairs of disembodied heads will it take?
How many detached hands and feet?
How many hollow cheeks, empty stomachs, vacant eyes?
How many skulls without memory?
He has been there, she has seen it, they have lived and died a long time.
He has something to say about who did what.
She has something to say about the living.
Let history honor the murmurs of conscience that are heard above ground.
Let praise flow to those who unclenched a fist.
Who granted men and women the freedom of the sparrow.
Who taught us to think twice.
Who showed us that famine is not a fast.
That exile is the last step.
That the rights of the few must be written down by the many.

She sees the leaves fly free.
He sees the wild horse and the sparrow.
Free to work, to consort with their kind, to choose or be chosen.
She sees them fed and feeding, mindful of the season.
He hears the continents shifting, she smells the air of change.
She tastes the wind-borne soot of rebirth.
He feels the human cry in his bones.

RALPH BLACK

21St Century Lecture

Listen. You know what a torn shirt
the world's become. You know how thin
its fabric. You know what seams are,
and how your life, as though by accident,
settles in and trembles them apart.
And everyone knows you don't mean it.
So you say to yourself, don't be stupid.
You say, don't sham and swindle your way
through these stark desecrations,
don't stand around as your body's
warming waters rise, as they lift
and pool around the trunks
of three hundred year old trees —
the ones that snatched away your breath
and all your words when you were a kid.
Your tea is getting cold. The shirts
you bought on a whim have to go back
to the Singapore sweatshop.
You're smart and caring enough, keening
over the paper each morning,
tuned in to just the right litany of fear —
Bagdad, Darfur, the Bronx —
the outstretched- or instantly severed hand.
You could turn the page from the steady
unraveling of the planet's bright threads.
But your throat rasps and freezes at the sight
of the Sea Lion sow chewing the face
off her newborn pup; at the Coho hatchlings
spilling out of the hatchery flume,
carrying their constellations of DNA
up and against the river's age-old equations;
at the polar bears starving at the edge
of their ice. You know the word *starving*,
you know the meaning of CO^2, you know
how apple seeds and smart bombs bloom,
how simple it is to flay a range of hills,
eviscerate a mountain with a spark.
You know how the stones can keep you warm.
You're not an idiot. You're not a fool.

You won't let your heart — that tiny,
glacial island — fracture and calve.
You think your love for your children
and your children's love for everything
but homework and spinach should be plenty.
The name of the wind is changing.
The wind, which you know is your breath,
and spills over flooded deltas, which churns
through the gleaming thickets of oil refineries,
fission factories, wind farms, water mills,
think tanks, smelters, grinders, brothels,
landfills, gun shops, billboards declaring
the newest-brightest-best — You know
how it fills you, how it lifts away from you
the words you use to talk back to yourself
late into the night. It's a very old wind, and you
utter it over and over, part mantra, part koan,
a playing-out of words like a old uncle spiraling
ten-pound test over his favorite run of rapids
thirty miles up the East Fork of that river
that spills now green and empty as an eye.
You know all this. No one's telling you anything
you haven't known for a hundred years.
But your tongue says *say it*, just the same.
Your mouth makes the shape of a call, a cry,
an uneven song. You reach for a pen,
tired as you are. You write it down, because
stories and maps are the same. You think
of the photograph you saw at the museum:
a ten year old boy born blind who lost
both his arms in his country's war.
He's at a desk, reading a book with his mouth.
He's leaning in and kissing the words,
in love with his own hunger.
He's doing with his whole body
everything he knows how to do.

DENISE DUHAMEL

David Lemieux

My first boyfriend is dead of AIDS. The one
who bought me a terrarium with a cactus
I watered until it became soft. The one

who took me to his junior high prom where I was shy
about dancing in public. The one who was mistaken
for a girl by a clerk when he wanted to try on a suit.

In seventh grade my first boyfriend and I looked a lot alike:
chubby arms, curly hair, our noses touching
when we tried our first kiss. My first boyfriend

was the only one who met my grandmother
before she died. Though, as a rule, she didn't like boys,
I think she liked my first boyfriend.

My first boyfriend and I sat in the back seat
of my mother's car, and on the ledge behind us
was a ceramic ballerina with a missing arm.

We were driving somewhere to have her repaired
or maybe to buy the right kind of glue.
My first boyfriend was rich and had horses

and airplanes he could fly by remote control.
My first boyfriend died on a mattress
thrown on the back of a pick-up

because the ambulance wouldn't come.
There was a garden in my first boyfriend's yard.
One day his mother said to us,

"Pick out some nice things for lunch."
My first boyfriend and I pulled at the carrot tops,
but all we came up with were little orange balls

that looked like kumquats without the bumps.
My first boyfriend and I heard ripping through the soil
that sounded close to our scalps, like a hair brush

through tangles. We were the ones who pushed
the tiny carrots back down, hoping they were able
to reconnect to the ground. We were the ones.

MARTÍN ESPADA

Litany at the Tomb of Frederick Douglass

Mount Hope Cemetery, Rochester, New York
November 7, 2008

This is the longitude and latitude of the impossible;
this is the epicenter of the unthinkable;
this is the crossroads of the unimaginable:
the tomb of Frederick Douglass, three days after the election.

This is a world spinning away from the gravity of centuries,
where the grave of a fugitive slave has become an altar.
This is the tomb of a man born as chattel, who taught himself to read in secret,
scraping the letters in his name with chalk on wood; now on the anvil-flat stone
a campaign button fills the O in Douglass. The button says: Obama.
This is the tomb of a man in chains, who left his fingerprints
on the slavebreaker's throat so the whip would never carve his back again;
now a labor union T-shirt drapes itself across the stone, offered up
by a nurse, a janitor, a bus driver. A sticker on the sleeve says: I Voted Today.
This is the tomb of a man who rolled his call to arms off the press,
peering through spectacles at the abolitionist headline; now a newspaper
spreads above his dates of birth and death. The headline says: Obama Wins.

This is the stillness at the heart of the storm that began in the body
of the first slave, dragged aboard the first ship to America. Yellow leaves
descend in waves, and the newspaper flutters on the tomb, like the sails
Douglass saw in the bay, like the eyes of a slave closing to watch himself
escape with the tide. Believers in spirits would see the pages trembling
on the stone and say: look how the slave boy teaches himself to read.
I say a prayer, the first in years: that here we bury what we call
the impossible, the unthinkable, the unimaginable, now and forever. Amen.

Riding by the Building Where
My Students Live on a Sunday

Nothing shatters.

The day around the prison gleams like the clean face of a spoon.

To the man on the bike beside me, I say, see how it blends in, the same brick and height, disappears after a mile like any other high-rise?

Only A. still sits inside, denied parole again for an assault twenty-three years ago.

And Officer M. sits in the Annex until ten, ordering the women's ID's according to his ideas of beauty.

The faster we go along the river, the more the city tips into background.

The blocks become ellipses, each building possibly a prison, possibly a warehouse full of pinwheels.

I want to stop longer.

But keep pedaling.

I tell myself prisons are inevitable and inevitably awful.

But don't believe this.

Beside us, the river is the streaming silver of dream hair.

Then the river, too, is behind us.

ELIOT KHALIL WILSON

Seven-Hundred Mile Fence

for Guillermo Martínez

Let the fence be
taller than our deepest free harbor,
a space-scraping net, hanging miles above our tallest statue
and as long and as long as a day in los campos.

They've been breeding and pouring over the border,
like a broken faucet of rusty water,
and gone are the places for swallowtails
and Western Whites.

But we've prayed, and now the government is clamping down
on the tide of undocumented Monarch butterflies,
closing the curtain by raising one.
The tongues of the wrinkled men

in the chamber of commerce
will rasp *Keep them all out,*
but their souls are hornet nests made of wadded dollars.
The wrinkled men want them in,

want to use them like shoes for their pale, tender feet,
want to see them stooped
in the furrows of the strawberry fields,
or with burning hands from the chili harvest,

or shingling the blistering roofs of Los Angles,
their brown backs reddening.
The wrinkled men want the families sleeping under farm trucks,
washing their laundry

in the stream below the country club.
And they want the blood of Guillermo Martínez,
caught between the fences and shot in the back by la migra.
M16s against a grape harvest knife and a bag

filled with envelopes and stamps.
This while coyotes and dogs trapped
between the fences are set free.

But up from El Rosario the Monarchs drift.

Call them a gang, call them all criminals
but no fence or gunship or law or razor wire
will stop their belonging. They belong.
See them like a boundless, shattered stained-glass window,

like hinges to unlockable doors.

ROBERT PRINGLE

A Station in Ohio

Below the brick house on the hill,
the creek turns softly south.
They can cross
except during spring rains.

Up the hill, a slave family,
through the Jonathan orchard —
south or north in America, 1857,
they are out of place.

Cellar door, after midnight,
no light, all are black;
trust warm as a handclasp,
fragile as apple buds at freezing.

Parents in standing room,
false wall of the coal bin;
mix of broken shoes, slate & chalk,
three children to a closet floor.

With the next new moon,
early for the usual harvests,
they will be taken deeper north
feeding a people desperate for home.

TOM HEALY

No Fear Of Fire

We are trees

and confess to nothing
in this ruckus of leaves
or its balancing catechism
of no sound.

No burden of trails,
no forestry
scratched into this hill,
nothing startled
from our underbrush.

Just the sun's unrooted gaze
jealous our thirst
has such glad color
and no fear of fire.

Let it come.

Rain will also come
and we are many.

And when questions come
from angrier landscapes,
answers will echo

in the laughter swirling
through our standing here

in promiscuous wind.

BARBARA HAMBY

Elizabeth Cady Stanton Writes the Dictionary

Even Susan thought I was too radical by half,
giving women the right to sue for divorce. Hush,
I said, it will all be ours one day. A beautiful (adj.)
knife, the mind, cutting through that Victorian drivel.
My brain and Susan's voice — we were an army (noun)
of two with thousands of foot soldiers. The backdrop
(q.v.) was the (art.) civil war, emancipation, and after
slaves were free, why not women? Marching got
us nothing, but black men got the vote. Universally (adv.)
we were screwed. Susan got back on her soapbox,
yelling about the vote, her one-note harangue . Chintz
armchairs were not for her, Quaker virago moving (verb)
countries into a time they could not, but for her, yet behold.

SEAN THOMAS DOUGHERTY

After the Election

what book is opened what hand-drawn pictures of saints what humble
shrouds ruby'd in the earth's flooded grief there in dog-hearted exile let
the roses sweep exhausted on the ground at the feet of the strikers crying
for bread in the poor drizzle against factory windows someone is sewing
the map of the world of what should be human with sound in the rooms
of bare bulbs in the unkempt child's hair in the mother's gold comb in
the music of trucks in the calling and the kiss like little trumpets there is
a love that is thick as the breath from loaves cooking in a crowded kitchen
where the amputees bow their heads to read the map that stops us from
lying a new life will enter like a long walk through the state of ruin to love
this city will celebrate 6:32 P.M. a boy raises his bicycle in the city of what
could be what should be he unrolls a map a red bicycle with silver rims
and he rides past cathedrals Italian-restaurants bodegas wheelchair-races
greenhouses cookie shops t'ai chi ballets in the parks where the jails have
been turned into print shops beauty parlors bakeries breathe the warm
bread on the kitchen table we have spread the map run our fingers over
the avenues of lentils the boulevards of sangria eggplant arroz chutney
couscous la conga in a bakery box in a blueberry muffin in the breaking
in the bowing in a bottle of milk in the newspaper where the pages are
blank and we lift our crayons with our new bodies where we draw like
umbilical cords like kite strings the lines that lead into the never known
mispronouncing the new words no one has yet to define this new gospel
crossing the last eclipse this cartography we claim toward a new refuge
this new passage rising into these houses of bread inside you.

PEGGY SHUMAKER

As War Goes On

Olive trees do not apologize.
Dusty, their uniforms
drop piece by piece

splattering the sidewalk.
No one can eat such fruit
without curing it in lye.

Brine. Oceans. Eyes.
Overflowing. Paper
beaten from sweat-

stained camouflage
shed by men ready
to be seen,

to speak. From the fountain
fresh waters. Vets beat
to a pulp

loosened fibers,
spread onto screens
the mash of their lives.

Soldiers so young
they've yet to bear
fruit, veterans

so old their roots
tangle, tap
rivers underground.

On the paper
we make of our lives
what shall we write?

For Phil, Hari, Drew ~ Iraq Veterans Against the War www.ivaw.org

*This poem grew from an experience with young veterans of the Iraq war. They travel the country and make combat paper from pieces of their old uniforms. They try to engage people in conversation about life during deployment and afterward

LINDSEY BROWN

The Clothesline Project

In summer, my mother hung my fathers' undershirts
out to dry. Once she held one in her hand, saying, "It smells
like the sun." In my bedroom, he never took it off — maybe

out of a sense of propriety, maybe out of convenience.
I always focused on the grooves
of the crew-neck collar waiting for them

to swallow me up. The moon peered
through the window, a giant
open eye. Now sixteen years later

arcs of t-shirts line the quad
as if a gypsy band set up camp on campus. A chalk-
colored after-

noon moon hangs in the sky. From a distance
the colors look
festive as carnival balloons: blue, red, pink, orange.

Here their muteness is power. Their brightness
echoes louder than clapping hands. Red and orange
for rape survivors; yellow,

battered women; child-sized blue shirts say "incest happened here." Look
closely. Colors speak.
Colors cry

out in the billowing wind. I reach
for a t-shirt the length
of my forearm from collar to seam,

can hear my own tears in its blue as
I hang it next to the others
for more than the moon to see.

JAKE ADAM YORK

Vigil

The bike, the handlebars, the fork,
spoked wheels still spinning off sun,

still letting go his weight as he
lay in the grass along Docena Road

just hours after the bomb went off
under the church steps downtown,

four girls dead, though they hadn't heard,
Virgil with a bullet in his heart, Virgil Ware

who wanted a bike for a paper-route
who perched on his brother's handlebars

and caught the white boys' bullet
but never got a bike or a headstone

or a 14th birthday, Virgil and his brother
and the bike in the grass off Docena Road.

The handlebars, fork, and iron diamond
frame that held them both, warming

in the Alabama sun. Stars of paint and chrome
that rained all over north Birmingham,

up and down the Docena-Sandusky road,
nesting like crickets in the weeds.

And the seat, wearing at the edges,
the cushion opening like a cattail

to the wind. But the frame, still holding
handed down and down and down

till bright as a canna. Then laid
with its brothers in a tangle in the sun.

Then gathering heat and darkening.
Then weeds insinuating the fork,

the sprocket, the pedal, each iron artery,
working back toward the light.

Let their flowers open from the mouths
of the handlebars and the seat-post.

Let them be gathered from the frame
and the frame raised up. Let it be

hot to the touch. Let its rust burn
into the finest creases of the hand

and the warp of the shirtsleeve and the pants
and worked into the temples' sweat.

Then let it descend into the furnace like a hand
that opens all its rivers, each tribute,

each channel, each buried town.
Let it gather this heat, this fire, hold it all.

Let the crucible door open like a mouth
and speak its bloom of light, molten and new.

Let me stand in its halo. Let me stand
as it pours out its stream of suns.

Let me gather and hold it like a brother.
And let it burn.

MARGARET ROZGA

Where Lawrence Learns the Law

South 50th Street

Cops were always parked right
in front of the Freedom House.
Saying there were threats against us.
They had to protect us.

Yeah, they protecting us,
but we the only ones going to jail.
One night, they arrested a girl
for throwing her cigarette on the sidewalk.

We went outside to see what was going on,
they arrested us, too. Took us downtown.
Fingerprinted us. Photographed us.
Yeah, for dropping a cigarette.

So we had to return the favor, right?
Drove out to Chief Breier's house
I'll never forget that address.

We parked in that all-white neighborhood,
sat out there all night. Guarding the Chief of Police.
Hey, there'd been threats against him.
We didn't want anything to happen to him.

Next night we're out there again.
What thanks do we get?
We're arrested
for guarding the chief of police
without a private detective's license.

SHERMAN ALEXIE

The Museum of Tolerance

has opened its doors
and, as agreed, we forgive all sins.

We check our coats
and regretfully remember
the twentieth century: War, war, war, war
followed closely by manned space flight.

I have the sudden urge to telephone old girlfriends and apologize!

This is the Museum of Tolerance: one room
with its one exhibit placed on a white satin pillow
which rests comfortably on an antique maple chair.

The exhibit: a small, red stone.

What does it mean? The debate begins simply enough
but adjectives and adverbs soon fill the room.

A man says, "If I am going to love somebody
then she must love me first."

Flashbulbs, the whir of advancing film.

The Museum of Tolerance, thank God, is open all night
but nobody can agree on the price of admission.

TIM SEIBLES

The Debt

I have the blood of the conquerors in my veins
and the blood of the enslaved and the slaughtered,
so where shall I rest with this
mixed river of blood painting my heart — what city
wants me, which woman will touch my neck?

So the Ivory Coast is sleeping in the angles
of my skull, and maybe two small French towns,
one in each leg, are also sleeping — and of course,
the first people in this land, with their long
black, black hair, seven of them
are napping along my ribs

                        and with all these people
adrift in my body, I am asleep as well —
dreaming their good wishes, their strained whispers —
sleepwalking all over America.
But it's all right; in America everyone
is asleep: at the wheel, on the job, even
with their fingers on the trigger, asleep
with their distant continents, the glittering
silence of their shattered histories
and the long pull of a thousand
thousand moons inside them.

                        They don't remember
how once we swam inside our mothers, that
once our mothers floated inside their mothers,
just as their mothers once waited inside those
before them and before that it was the same —
all the way back to the first mother
in Africa,

            that slim, short, quick-tempered woman
whose children crawled

all over the planet, then got big and started
hurting each other — with the conquerors

in their bright armor, trying to finish everything.

I know where the blame falls. I know
I could twist my brown skin, my mixed nations, my
kinky hair into a fist. I know.   I know.

But I hear a stranger music in my bones —
the windy shimmer of long fields, the singular tree
of all blood rising, a quiet of birds stunned by dusk,
the future awake singing from these wounds, and

what is the lesson of history, it not
that we owe each other more bread, more
friendship, fewer lies,
less cruelty.

KEVIN CLARK

Elizabeth at Seabrook

— nuclear power protests, 1977

Even today, brushing blush on my cheeks,
I can re-imagine the turning face
Of that young guardsman irradiated
By dawn sun or the fissured power plant.
He said, Ma'am, you know my orders: It's time
To separate the men from the women.
One afternoon walk I'd seen a flower
Arranged in a Fibonacci sequence
Of new helical rays. What was its name?
The artist says beauty walks math spirals
Out past numbers, out past all reason.
That's a moment to live for, isn't it?
On the damp armory floor, the men sat
In circles, then the women around them.
At the center were piled our tied shoes.
We were surrounded by a tight square
Of masked soldiers holding shields, Billy clubs.
I stood to tell the lieutenant of our
Consensus pact: The instant a guardsman
Touches any one of our group, every
Man and woman will strip naked. Like that,
Rouge shadows blossomed on his cheeks the way
A thumb touch might shame any fresh petal
Into darkness. Their retreat took seconds.
Then we sat alone in the new silence.
I had always believed that peace was won
Unarmed in the face of odds. Who could know
Naked skin would send them into shadow.
They gave up and let us out. For two days
I slept and dreamed. At first the nuke sent up
A mushroom cloud. Then night, distant voices,
My mother, a ring of linked friends, moonlight.
I'm strolling through the wetlands, alone,
Wearing only my hiking boots. The sucking
Muck holds steps like kisses. Fibonacci
Florets billow in the sky. When I wake,
That flower's lost name burns me alive.

Rest

Sabbath is a river that flows
every day but Sunday,
yet there is no rest
from war.

The velocity
of its ferocious light
is its maximum possible velocity,
even in the spired
faculty of the soul
with all her longing and avidity.

Bitter in the belly
but honey in the mouth ~
copious resin of experience ~
are these *cryptonyms, influentials.*

Firmly rooted as dogwoods, as axioms,
each star casts about again
for more of its core to burn

while below,
our sole garden is italicized
by crime, the first and last of things:

Justice is conflict,
not the other way around.

MARTHA COLLINS

Birmingham

Because after I'd seen the church where it
was bombed where the four bodies were stacked
on top of each other said Josephine Marshall
Tuskegee '33 she saw nothing
but bloody sheets

> *laundry couldn't be washed*
> *in the same machines*

and read about this City of Churches this Magic
City this Bombingham where Shuttlesworth's
church and house had been bombed where Chambliss
before that Sunday had bombed homes for twenty
years where because of *Brown* the Klan castrated
a man who'd done nothing not even looked
at a white woman in '57

> *couldn't read a book*
> *about black and white rabbits*

because after I'd seen the two fountains the
replicated streetcar classroom courtroom the actual
door of that Birmingham Jail cell and followed
the tapes of the sit-ins the kneel-ins the marches
the students the children the hoses the dogs
and listened again to the famous speech

> *couldn't be sworn in*
> *on the same Bible*

the museum led to a hall they called it
Procession Hall where simply to walk was to join
the life-sized marchers because I had sat in a classroom
had only read the papers when it happened

SONJA LIVINGSTON

The First Gulf War

It must have been all the rage
the year I pushed myself into tight jeans and
squeezed through the metal doors of the federal building, stormed
down the halls with eleven other comrades. The Senator wasn't in,
just his secretary, someone's grandma, who held a hand to her chest and said she wasn't sure
she should buzz us through, so that we had no choice but press
twelve faces against the glass and promise not to make trouble, promise anything
to have her open the door so we could get inside and protest
according to plan. We'd met for weeks, after all, hashing out the event —
Would there be signs? Yes! In case of handcuffs, how best to resist?
Softly. Think babies falling from mother's arms — not to mention the fever
started by the red-haired homeschooler over consistent life ethic,
No, we said, *we're Catholic, but only so much*
and the session spent letting down the kid whose mother
didn't want his college applications sullied with arrest, war was war, God knew,
but her boy was just starting out, until finally the day came and our lady
of the hidden buzzer wrung her hands and searched the black office for clues
until trust got the better of her and she said *well, I suppose if it's just a package* and a foot
and few elbows later, we all got in, the D'Amato Dozen,
we called ourselves the next day on the news, after sitting
in for hours to condemn injustice in the Gulf
and as we sat singing Cat Stevens
songs I felt the secretary rattling behind us, thinking of the bus
she'd missed, her husband's dinner, or what the Senator
might say, she probably made seven bucks
an hour, our hostage, whose voice had cracked
on her call to the police, who sat tearing
at her fingernails, making angels
of folded coffee filters
while we sang *Peace*
Train and, in the end, the handcuffs were little more than twist-ties,
the paddy wagon; spacious, my hair; still fresh, the cop who snapped
my picture; interested, and the woman
from the Senator's office; flushed
and fishing a key from her pocketbook
with trembling slivered fingers

SAM HAMILL

True Peace

Half broken on that smoky night,
hunched over sake in a serviceman's dive
somewhere in Naha, Okinawa,
nearly fifty years ago,

I read of the Saigon Buddhist monks
who stopped the traffic on a downtown thoroughfare
so their master, Thich Quang Dúc, could take up
the lotus posture in the middle of the street.
And they baptized him there with gas
and kerosene, and he struck a match
and burst into flame.

That was June, nineteen-sixty-three,
and I was twenty, a U.S. Marine.

The master did not move, did not squirm,
he did not scream
in pain as his body was consumed.

Neither child nor yet a man,
I wondered to my Okinawan friend,
what can it possibly mean
to make such a sacrifice, to give one's life
with such horror, but with dignity and conviction.
How can any man endure such pain
and never cry and never blink.

And my friend said simply, "Thich Quang Dúc
had achieved true peace."

And I knew that night true peace
for me would never come.
Not for me, Nirvana. This suffering world
is mine, mine to suffer in its grief.

Half a century later, I think
of Bô Tát Thich Quang Dúc,
revered as a bodhisattva now — his lifetime

building temples, teaching peace,
and of his death and the statement that it made.

Like Shelley's, his heart refused to burn,
even when they burned his ashes once again
in the crematorium — his generous heart
turned magically to stone.

What is true peace, I cannot know.
A hundred wars have come and gone
as I've grown old. I bear their burdens in my bones.
Mine's the heart that burns
today, mine the thirst, the hunger in the soul.

Old master, old teacher,
what is it that I've learned?

INDRAN J. AMIRTHANAYAGAM

After Battle

Call me a fool to bow before Myth,
rotund, middle-aged, framed with cubs,
to believe in rights derived from soil
and birth, to think my voice will be heard

while guns blast away. There is one truth
I would like to share. The dictator knows
it more than fellow residents on earth,
listening to pounding on the door

from a faithful aide-de-camp
who says Swiss bankers are releasing
names of deposit holders,
a single engine plane

rumbles outside the window,
come away, Man, run
with your pockets filled
and hands free, with your wife

and children, pockets filled
and hands free, your speech
tucked in the inside sleeve
delivered at Oxford in glad

and misguided youth that said,
when pressed against the sea wall,
blindfolded, punched in the stomach
left to wait for a bullet,

especially then, show compassion,
love your enemy, pirouette,
mix your blood with the earth,
become a stain in the heart,

a voice in sleep, a memory
that insists on rising with the sun,
in the crying of fowl, growl
of an armoured convoy

like thunder and rain
until the monsoon returns
to the sea and babies' milk
curdles again left out

in this unforgiving heat,
tickling ant song,
peace beyond
understanding

of craters and graves,
hulks of schoolbuses,
spit of sand between
lagoon and sea.

CLAUDIA CARLSON

After Ice and Rain

Jackhammers in the spring
sidewalks are reborn

the damp squares enticing
transgressive footprints and initials

they dry into new canvasses
for spent gum and skateboard skids

until Hani the street artist comes
and scrapes them clean

chalk lines blossom
across the sandy surfaces

heros are drawn, Obama, Hilary Clinton,
Michael Jackson, Sonia Sotomayor...

among the putti and familiar saints,
a glory of new colors emerge.

SOPHIA KARTSONIS

Cisterna

Well
Sister
there
will
be
water.

What are
those well-
wishers waiting to be?
Tell them you are already sister
to the meadow's meadowness, the song's songing. Will
you ask them where they're headed, then tell them *you're already there.*

There will be water there.
There will be water.
There will
be well
enough alone enough for all and thirsters
everywhere will drink and drink and be

well. Believe
me when I tell you there
are miracles and there are miracles. We saw you, Sister
Extravagance, walk on water. Whatever
weighed heavy only buoyed you then. You knew about well-
being when you hardly felt the will

to be. You are the living will
of every dragonfly, you worship the bee
and his honey-ache. You've known it well.
The honeysuckle that drew him there
is called Kissing-by-the-Gate. This body of yours is mostly water.
This body, Sister,

is called a field. This field, Sister,
has known floods and fires and maintains will
over the succulents and drinks up on holy water
every drop. Who blesses the kneeling bee,

his church of being? Our offering of pennies rolled down a hill.
The wishing well,
the tithing, the copper cargo that paves the cellar of throat where there

gleams this knowing: We will be sisters and resisters.
There are transistor
radios singing from the well, all this is radiating. The flower is a given.
The water is given. We are given. We are given over.

SARAH CEDEÑO

Vitamin D and Frisbees

While your father researches clinical trials, you "Google" celebrities who suffer
from Multiple Sclerosis: Montell Williams. Joan Didion. Richard Pryor. Smile
when you miss the stop sign on a street you've driven down
since you were seventeen. Smile when you dump your coffee
on the laminated floor in your classroom. Smile when you run into walls,
your skin bruised like an old piece of fruit. Smile when you throb
until you're doubled-over. Smile when you break down in your husband's arms
after missing an antidepressant. Don't believe
this is a relapse. Have faith everyone has moments like this.
Smile at four AM, when your infant son wails with swollen gums,
and your head spikes with pain like lightening.
Your sister makes a profile on the official MS website.
It becomes a fan club, a topic for coffee at the kitchen table. Almost
a cult. Friends and family want you to walk for the Rochester MS walk.
This provides hope, which your family members need, more than you do.
"Want me to sponsor a team?" your father asks, "I could win a
frisbee. Maybe even a gift certificate to that new Italian restaurant." He won't
stop joking. He's become an encyclopedia of facts, "You know, lack
of Vitamin D is linked to MS. There's no sun, no D, in Rochester." You are pale,
and so you try to connect the two. But it is bright outside the day you walk.
All your friends and family walk. Everyone walks. Look around:
a jacketed toddler, holding an adult's hand, plods on. Realize
the unfair way reality manifests itself — with others
rocking on canes from the sidelines or pushing on in wheel
chairs to raise funds that help themselves, and others, to stand. That is when you
hear the footsteps begin. And they keep going, and you imagine
they're half around the world already, echoing still.

DAVID BAKER

The Spring Ephemerals

Here she comes with her face to be kissed. Here she comes
lugging two plastic sacks looped over her arms and stuffed

with fresh shoots. It's barely dawn. She's been out
for an hour already, digging up what she can save

before developers raze the day's lot sites and set woodpiles
ablaze. That's their plan for the ninety-plus acres.

She squats in the sun to show me wild phlox
in pink-running-to-blue, rue anemone, masses

of colt's foot, wild ginger, blood root and may-
apples, bracken and fiddlehead fern — ferns being not

spring ephemerals per se, but imperiled by road graders
come to shave the shaded slopes where they grow.

Once I held her in a snow cover of sheets. Wind beat
the world while we listened. Her back was a sail,

unfurling. She wanted me to touch stitches there,
little scabs, where doctors had sliced the sick cells

and cauterized her skin for safety's sake.
Now her hands are spotted by briars, bubbles of blood

daubed in brown. She's got burrs in her red hair.
Both sleeves are torn. She kneels as the sunlight

cuts through pine needles above us, casting a grid
like the plats the surveyors use. It's the irony

of every cell: that it divides to multiply.
This way the greedy have bought up the land

behind ours to parcel for resale at twenty-
fold what they paid weeks ago.

It's a race to outrun their gas cans and matches,
to line the path to our creek with transplants

of spice bush, yellow fawn lily, to set aside space
in the garden for the frail. She adjusts the map

she's drawn of the tumbling woods — where each
flower and fern come from, under what tree, beside

which ridge. *Dysfunctional junctional nevus*:
a name like a bad joke for the growth on her skin,

pigment too pale for much sunlight. *Drooping trillium*,
she says, handing me a cluster of roots, unfolding leaves —

rare around here. How delicate, a trillium,
whose oils are food for ants, whose sessile leaves are

palm-sized, tripartite. They spread a shadow over
each stem's fragile one bloom, white in most cases,

though this one's maroon. This makes it rarer.
It hangs like a red bell safe from the sun. It bends

like our necks bend, not in grief, not prayer,
as we work with our backs to the trees, as they burn.

RIGOBERTO GONZÁLEZ

Response to the Sidewalk Preacher

We've heard it all before: that the earth
will fold its arms into a knot
and squeeze out our cries with confessions; that the sea
will suck its saliva back in,
mimicking the thirsty mouths of the dead; that the sky
will put out its flame in one breath
and we'll prick our eyes shut in the dark;
that we'll take off our souls, those dirty shirts,
and our hearts will crack like hot glass in the cold.
All this tomorrow. Over and over, tomorrow.

Well, why not today? Already
the moon hovers like the inner curve of an empty bowl; already
the sun burns a hole through our tongues; already
the streets, those malpractice surgeons, cut us to halves
with their needles and knives and stand at the corner
to buy a cup of our diluted blood; already
a death certificate is a welfare check; already
we value sleeping pills like teeth; already
we wear our skins like potato sacks
and keep fingers in our pockets like tarnished spoons.

Give me that book in your hand. I'll eat it
like a sandwich; I'll sleep on it
like a mother's lap and empty my ear of bad dreams;
I'll hold it up to bandage the sky; I'll throw it
into the air and let it drop its faith like rain; I'll wear it
like a hat and tip it like a cornucopia.
If it's true what you say, preacher, that this book
holds the answers between its ribs, let me have it.
I'll chew through the bone, I'll get to the center,
I'll swallow it, I'll crush it like a third lung.

D. A. POWELL

[listen mother, he punched the air:
I am not your son dying]

a stabat mater

listen mother, he punched the air: I am not your son dying
the day fades and the starlings roost: a body's a husk a nest of goodbye

his wrist colorless and soft was not a stick of chewing gum
how tell? well a plastic bracelet with his name for one. & no mint
his eyes distinguishable from oysters how? only when pried open

she at times felt the needle going in. felt her own sides cave. she rasped
she twitched with a palsy: tectonic plates grumbled under her feet

soiled his sheets clogged the yellow BIOHAZARD bin: later to be burned
soot clouds billowed out over the city: a stole. a pillbox hat [smart city]
and wouldn't the taxis stop now. and wouldn't a hush smother us all

the vascular walls graffitied and scarred. a clotted rend in the muscle
wend through the avenues throttled t-cells. processional staph & thrush

the scourge the spike a stab a shending bile the grace the quenching
mother who brought me here, muddler: open the window. let birds in

The Battle of Nashville

Snow gives the sky a new dimension — depth,
a soft glow, as if the air lit the yard,
which slopes to the city, which shimmers.
The river is always moving, but the atrium
on Fifth, the Kress, where blacks locked arms
and would not budge. A plow takes the hill,
where cars line up in rows, and half-built lofts
replace the houses. The man who built our house
built diesel engines, and kept the trucks
he couldn't fix. His daughters sold it all,
except the how-to books, the shop fan
he left in the attic. We're not brave,
but we find each other in bed at night,
your hand or my hand reaching out.
In the morning, you take the trash, and I make
the coffee. Nearby, battles were fought,
and men, whose wives waited for them, died.
If soldiers held the highest ground, one stood
here. If there is one, there is at least
one more. Standing shoulder to shoulder,
they share a blanket, as snow settles in the trees.
I think they are afraid. I think this is love.

RODNEY JONES

Doing Laundry

Here finally I have shriven myself and am saint,
Pouring the detergent just so, collating the whites
With the whites, and the coloreds with the coloreds,

Though I slip in a light green towel with the load
Of whites for Vivian Malone and Medgar Evers,
Though I leave a pale shift among the blue jeans

For criminals and the ones who took small chances.
O brides and grooms, it is not always perfect.
It is not always the folded, foursquare, neat soul

Of sheets pressed and scented for lovemaking,
But also this Friday, stooping in a dark corner
Of the bedroom, harvesting diasporas of socks,

Extracting like splinters the T-shirts from the shirts.
I do not do this with any anger, as the poor chef
May add to a banker's consommé the tail of a rat,

But with the joy of a salesman closing a sweet deal,
I tamp loosely around the shaft of the agitator
And mop the kitchen while it runs the cycles.

Because of my diligence, one woman has time
To teach geography, another to design a hospital.
The organ transplant arrives. The helicopter pilot

Steps down, dressed in an immaculate garment.
She waves to me and smiles as I hoist the great
Moist snake of fabric and heave it into the dryer.

I who popped rivets into the roof of a hangar,
Who herded copper tubes into the furnace,
Who sweated bales of alfalfa into the rafters

High in the barn loft of July, who dug the ditch
For the gas line under the Fourteenth Street overpass
And repaired the fence the new bull had ruined,

Will wash the dishes and scrub the counters
Before unclogging the drain and vacuuming.
When I tied steel on the bridge, I was not so holy

As now, taking the hot sheets from the dryer,
Thinking of the song I will make in praise of women,
But also of ordinary men, doing laundry.

Walking at the U.N.

This afternoon, I visit a friend,
a deputy of the European Commission.
We walk in the U.N. rose garden.
(Last time I was here, it was opened
to the public. He explains since Sept. 11th,

the gardens have only been accessible
to U.N. employees and their guests.)
The sun burns like a wick in our conversation
and, later, in the unpredictable current of the river.
How from island to island people bound in nations

find their way, even as the unparsed narratives
of the conquered and vanquished more often do not.
In the presence of my enemy.
You are a skillful scalawag to my American
parched corn, but we both have read our Donne

and Paine and malice is not a binder
or a virtue in our shared rubric. Writing
more specifically Poetry lies at the elemental
core of democracy. By definition, it seeks a foundation
for the commonwealth in the truth

of the individual, guaranteed and restored
through the integrity of language.
New poets often stand in the midst of old stones
envisioning a new way; are, after all,
themselves a part of this tallow world.

LAURA KASISCHKE

World Peace

A day like a mayfly on which someone slammed a Bible, all

exoskeletal radiance and insignificance in the dark. We find

ourselves the only
mother and child
who decided it was wise in this storm-impending crisis

to come to the County Fair.

Sheep among strangers. One
lone pony tethered to a pole. The prize
pig speaks eloquently in his sleep
on the tired subject or world peace, and the devil

who owns all this fairness outright
sits in a chair over there
by the fence
and lets his dog sniff around at the air. Briefly

it's air
made from the kind of paper
the repo-men roll through the halls of the house
to keep the mud on their boots from ruining your rugs
on the day they stomp
in and out
with all the things you ever bought on credit,
which, in the end, was everything you had:

As my grandma used to say,
We're going to have some weather.

But, at the moment, like petals —
a soft spray of spit, we are made of it.
And love, that slut, just

runs around deep-kissing everyone. So why

are we blind

to her wild suppositions
ninety-nine percent of the time?

Or does love generally never love us quite this much?

Well, might it suffice to say today I am struck dumb
by the laughable notion of numbers,

the whole hilarious idea of *greed*?
And the absurdity of feeling anything but peace
flies right over my head
like a flock of alarm clocks on the breeze.

Yes, Grandma, *God rest your soul*, we
will definitely have some weather,

but, for now,
the rides are quiet, the fun house is free, there are
no lines,

and at every gate a patient man or woman waits
for our tickets
with an open hand and a smile.

ANNE PANNING

Take Back the Night

It's cold in upstate New York, even in October. Still,
we march down our town's narrow streets
with candles in hand: a long, lingering light

show of women, children, and exactly two men. A cardboard sign
is shoved into my mittened hand: NO MEANS NO!
I pump it high into the sky

like a union man on strike. Barb's daughter, Savoy, holds the banner
in front: WOMEN UNITE! Gold satin words
on purple batik lift in the wind, then fall.

My student, Lindsay, shuffles behind me
and I hear her tender voice: *However we dress, wherever we go, yes means yes
and no means no!* I struggle to find the rhythm

of the words, but my eight year old son pulls at my arm.
"I'm cold," he says. "My legs are tired!"
"Yes," I say, "I know. But this is important. Someday

you'll see why." But his needs are more immediate.
He carries his own little sign: HEY-HEY,
HO-HO, PATRIARCHY HAS GOT TO GO!

As we wind down Main Street, a car full of thumping bass
lays on the horn before snarling off. Inside
the brightly lit diner, families peek out at our spectacle.

A teenaged girl pounds the glass, and waves.
Her father lifts his coffee cup to us, in toast. Afterwards,
there is pizza in the fireside lounge. A rape victim speaks

passionately of survival; I watch my son listen.
This is *not* about violence, she says.
This is not about violence at all.

Miss Sealy

High-busted and small,
she ran her school
for model whites.

When blacks bussed in
what seemed to her
a sampling of poor,
low reading scores,

she stood at the door
protecting her wards.

The hushed, dark children
wary of hate
looked at their mothers

and the model school,
at old Miss Sealy
huffing and small

standing guard
against the door,

and wondered at
her shallow skin
whose depth of white
would let them in.

The Deaf Manifesto

At Vasemblye square they make us sit on our hands. Caught signing, we are arrested. We meet in public toilets to feel each other's throats, we close doors, turn on flashlights, and sign. The deaf hand functions as mouth — thumb as tongue, fingers are lips.

Prisons at Tedna St. are called "Centers for Encouragement of the Deaf to Hear." Officials say arresting us prevents the epidemic. They suspect we possess no speech; speech, the only barrier that separates them from the animals. Colonialism moves its mouth: children are not permitted silence before speech forces their lips. They open lips. We move hands. Human beings need silence but cannot have it.

You are alive, I whisper to myself, therefore something in you listens

something runs down the street, falls, fails to get up. I run, etcetera, with my legs and my hands, etcetera, I run down Vasenka street, etcetera, it only takes a few minutes to make a man.

JULIE SOPHIA PAEGLE

Latvian Boys' Choir

Between 1988 and 1991, Latvians, Estonians, and Lithuanians held protests against Soviet occupation in which the singing of banned folk songs played a prominent role. The Singing Revolution was instrumental in the Baltic States' independence from Soviet Occupation.

— So many wrists, such a short life
lodged in that part of the arm, held

stiffly at the side of song; such a brief
respite between breath and forte — Wild

lean notes of aria tunnel the air between
the boys' small bodies: bodies of wrist

and of song, bodies gasped and wished and hinting
the steady risen rapture of the Riga Dome —

conjured and convincing, staggered on the stairs
before the single flashing hand of the metronome —

and eleven years (their lifetime!) after their amethyst
shore glowed from Tallinn to Vilnius and the prayers

of their parents who assembled — two million strong —
and sang — human chain in occupation — their songs.

ESTHA WEINER

THE NEWS, New Year's Eve, 1999

We watch him
light one candle, then step
outside his former prison cell,
offer the candle
to his successor
in the new South Africa.

We watch choreographed bodies
move down the corridor
past the cages
with their doors flung open,
free now
to dance on Robben Island,
to leap
beyond the flames.

DEREK MONG

Flying is Everything I Imagine Now and More

No shudder, no plunge, no cabin
                              strafed by sun

as when the earth constricts these wingtips and pulls
us like a bowstring
                         below the cloudline; no
intercom or ice storm, no seatbelt signs lit

like a thought
 achieved in chorus; no red-eyes

trembling like cross hairs on the horizon;
no threat, no glance met
                              (as has been endemic
these last six years) by a fear that does nothing

but unite us —
                    no flying really scares me now

save this scenario I've loved too long
and replayed
                    at those altitude where clouds still
canopy imagination: it begins

with the cabin pressure bled
      all over states

already red, till each passenger hovers,
tethered
            to his seat buckles or pursuing
chewing gum, hands parting the breathing cups

like seaweed —
                    But stop. See my problem? I want

so badly to recast in-flight disaster
as gorgeous, that whoosh
                              of air narrowing where

an exit clasp detached and heaven gasps me

back into the ether,
                    even roll my limbs

in its mouth a spell before the earth draws back
on the distance
                    I tried to put between us.
There's reason here, and a few good intentions

lost as this fall blurs
            into the after-life

it's hurtling after: there's my plane sailing on,
there's its jetstream
        of color-coded worry
trailing the tail-fin. I watch my clothes gently

lift away till I'm pale
        as a lightning bolt

and the chutes of rain I've punched through nimbus clouds
chase me
        toward the cause of all this desperate
imagination: it's these streets and crowds

looming larger now
and wholly literal

about all that they're afraid of. I once hoped
to ease the sky
                    within our reach, imagine
our recent victimhood as so much fuel burned

up in transit. But what can lyric
                    say to fear

hijacking countries? Only this, the lowest
point I can imagine:
                    I'm falling, arms out,
through smog, the dust splitting up till I'm costumed

in the exhaust
            of my neighbors. I see cities

aglow like circuit boards, and cars lighting paths
from one target
                    to another. A noise picks
up like a thousand screens, and I whisper

into that music:
                    America, I am

so harmless now, spilling down perpetually
toward you. Draw
                    your sunroofs back and call me
home. Let your grass blades raise their heads to meet me.

M GIOIA

Rookery Mockery

When I read that the gay penguins split up, I laughed
at myself, at my silly sadness over bird gossip.

Opponents declared victory: nature is heterosexual.
The gay otters, swimming hand in hand, declined to comment.

How absurd and tragic for the penguin left behind,
with only fish for comfort. Animals know loneliness.

Still we all bear that scar; life is endless migration.
Even caged penguins feel its echo. Examined, it yields no new questions.

Wonder, instead, over the one who returned to normal
life with the spare, dry cruelty of the desperate.

I might be wrong. Penguin emotion is elusive.
His could be a noble pronouncement: Fall in Love and Do The Right Thing.

But perhaps his choice was for windows unbroken.
Nuclear family dinners. No death threats.

When his struggle is over, love and body
protected by law, no beatings or civil unions — how giddy the relief.

Or maybe he wonders if it was worth the price, this simplicity.
If he would rather fight. If he went willing.

Like all queer animals he is never himself, only a representative.
A ghost façade, the slim shadow of possibility between white and black.

So silly, that hope, as easily popped as the laugh
bubbles that gather under the ribs, bruising that not-heart spot.

PATRICK BIZZARO

Not on The Rez

for Antonio

My part-Cherokee wife gave birth to our
part-Cherokee son, he, a fraction himself
of the fraction she is. Slow genocide,
this dilution of pure blood. My wife

measured by that uncertain fraction she
is told to use to measure herself. Our
son only part of that. Me, none. But his-
torical guilt burns through my blood. If she

recognizes a name on the Dawes Roll,
she makes me more the intruder I am. She
alone knows for sure who she is and not
in Indian blood, but in Indian

ways, not on the Rez but on the trail she
walks in tears, carrying this cause, you know,
this reason for her life, this tie others
in her family would deny. My son, our son,

named at the ceremony of his birth
for powerful eagles with more native ties,
is raised to respect the right things, to
pause before difference, to see himself.

NAOMI SHIHAB NYE

Those Whom We Do Not Know

To feel the love of people whom we love is a fire that
feeds our life. But to feel the affection that comes from
those whom we do not know . . . is something still greater
and more beautiful . . .
                                        — *Pablo Neruda*

1.

Because our country has entered
into war, we can have
no pleasant pauses anymore —

instead, the nervous turning
one side to another,
each comer crowded by the far
but utterly particular
voices of the dead,

of trees, fish, children,
calling, calling,
wearing the colorful plastic shoes
so beloved in the Middle East,
bleeding from the skull,
the sweet hollow along the neck.

I forget why. It's been changed.
For whatever it was
we will crush the vendor
who stacked sesame rings
on a tray
inside the steady gaze
of stones.
He will lose his balance
after years of perfect balance.

Catch him! Inside every sleep
he keeps falling.

2.

I support all people on earth
who have bodies like and unlike my body,
skins and moles and old scars,
secret and public hair,
crooked toes. I support
those who have done nothing large,
sifter of lentils, sifter of wisdoms,
speak. If we have killed no one
in the name of anything bad or good,
may light feed our leafiest veins.

I support clothes in the wash-kettle,
a woman stirring and stirring
with stick, paddle, soaking out grime,
simple clothes the size of bodies
pinned to the sky.

3.

What we learned left us.
None of it held.

Now the words ignite.
Slogans knot around necks
till faces bulge.

Windows of sand, doorways,
sense of shifting .
each time you blink —

that dune? Used to be
a house. And the desert
soaking up echoes —

those whom we did not know
think they know us now.

CHARLES JENSEN

In Laramie

I'll keep loving all I'm given to
love, there's no other revenge.
                    — Christopher Davis

The body is
taken from the roadside strap.

The hewn ties
knotted at the wrists are the worst kind of lie:

the body
of the boy has been removed from its post

like a sandbag,
heavy and limp, clotted with bits of dried grass.

I lay him
across my lap.

I stroke
his blood-soaked hair with my cold hand.

He smells
not human, but machine — the copper of his body is not alive.

My body,
mechanical in its care of him, shudders like clockwork gears, but

I'll keep loving
all I'm given. There's no other gift.

The boy
is taken from my arms. There's no revenge for losing this,

no mistake.
There's no remaking what is lost, and yes —

there's
no other love.

PATRICIA JABBEH WESLEY

Ghosts Don't Go Away Just Like That

Sometimes they lurk in hallways where they have lost
the other side of them. They may hover over new havocs

like the ones that carried them away from their bodies,
the ones that caused them to lose themselves in that rush.

Ghosts don't go away just like that, you know; they
come in that same huge crowd that was massacred

together with them, and since that massacre may have
happened at school, in a bar or at church, they

can be found, kneeling at the pulpit, singing and taking
communion again and again, with everyone else.

They gather on a Saturday evening, as the sun sets over
the hills and a small flash of yesterday's lightening lingers

from that old storm as the new storm rides in, and then,
there they are, ghosts; you can see them only if you have

eyes to see them as ghosts of humans, and yet not ghosts.
They're looking to see if we will recall that they were here.

To see if we will build a stone to honor the fact that they
were here, with us, walking and talking, like us, to see

if we will remember that they lost so much blood
in the shooting, that they broke a leg or two, and that

so many of them were not counted in that sad number.
They want to know if we will put up a stone or keep

the fire burning to put out the fires, to stop all the killing
in the city streets, around the world, to stop

all the killings in the eyes of the city streets.

FADY JOUDAH

Garden

"Death makes angels of us all"
I'd written on the blackboard in the cadaver room

The next morning someone wrote "Are you sure?"
If not angels then flowers I said then flew

To the town of holy taverns
Where beggars prostrate for hours

Until one sits straight up head engorged like a lily
On fast-forward in a nature show

At the Bed-&-Breakfast the owner served us crab quiche
The nearby pueblo was closed that day

A mother kept shouting Go back Go back
So we rode a tour bus to the levee

"Mean ol' levee taught me to weep and moan"
The old man with crumby pockets snapped

"Son this lottery ticket's expired!
No matter here's some money for it"

"But if it wins dear sir" the hobo said
"Forget me not forget me not"

RENNY GOLDEN

Republic Steel Chicago South Works

I

In the heat of May 1937 my grandfather
sits in the grass of an industrial park
with hundreds of striking steelworkers.

Boy's kites throw diamond colors to a cobalt sky,
men tilt beer barrels, pitch horseshoes onto stakes
hammered by thick, calloused hands.

When the police circle that Memorial Day picnic, men form
lines, a sun-mottled army of white undershirts, red and black
suspenders. They move as one in front of their families.

Tension runs the line the way a bass pulls tight,
the hook tearing deeper and deeper.
The strikers wait for the circle of blue shirts to loosen.

When Captain Mooney orders the police circle to tighten
everyone bolts, a thunder of feet beat through wicker baskets,
plates of beans, sauerkraut, pig knuckles, fried chicken.

The shots split Leon Franchesco's faded workshirt,
a stain opening like a rose. Sam Popovitch, in his seventies, can't run.
He falls holding his smashed skull, his dying eyes astonished.

An accordian winces where they push Dolan from a line of shots.
Workers pull the fallen Sam Causey into someone's car
but cops drag him bleeding onto the street.

Otis Jones and nine others will not see the strike end.
Otis Jones' boy runs ahead, he does not see his father's crumpled body.
He looks up to see the kites fall slowly, crookedly toward blood.

II

Sixty years later we stand in the union hall near a bleached Republic Steel sign.
The hall creaks and moans, a ratty velvet curtain is backdrop for the speakers.
Ed Sadlowski says *We'll never forget what happened here.*

Old men clap, shift weight, raise trembling hands, sing *Solidarity Forever.*
The workers shuffle to the catered luncheon, eat pizza at dark tables,
then walk into the afternoon where once a pale sky

rained kites, helpless in the plundered air.

RICHARD MICHELSON

Gift Wrapping the Garbage

My father's gift-wrapping the garbage.
"Bee — you — tee — full," he says.
Four bundles, and his accent (Brooklyn)
wraps like a bow around each.

Eight days into the strike
and the world smells like soup.
"Kreplach soup," he says.
"Your Aunt Ida's.
Know what I mean?"

My son can't picture it —
the neighborhood,
its poverty —
and I've lost the point,
trying to explain myself.
"Poor," I'm yelling. "Poor."
And suddenly my eyes are popping
like Dangerfield's on Letterman,
until my son takes pity.
"OK," he asks, "how poor?"

"Laugh," my father says, "if you want to,
but don't *they* all love Christmas?"
His accent is on the they,
but weren't times different then?

It was a Jewish Neighborhood
and then it was a Negro neighborhood
until the Puerto Ricans drove out the Blacks.
Shvartzes, I used to say
and Schwartzes, would echo back.

"Stop talking garbage,"
my mother says, but
aren't I my father's son?

"Every problem," he taught me
"has a solution,"
and I've got to tell you, *they*
stole that garbage
lickety-split.

We danced together, clapping
like two comics
in a Catskill routine. Me, squealing
with my *kvitchadicker* voice
(high and squeaky),
as I held onto him,
held onto him,
tight.

"How tight," my son asks,
but just now I'm not in the mood
for his sarcasm. I'd rather weep.
I'd rather watch this old newsreel —
my father working himself to death,
I mean literally, and dying out on the street,
lying there, maybe an hour,
one   more   dead   Jew.

"Take out the damn garbage," I tell my son.
Sure, I'd rather hug him, but right now
isn't my heart on the roller coaster
at Coney Island, and I'm barely holding on?

JASON SCHNEIDERMAN

What You Know

I know you know what it looked like, that you watched
it on television, the way even those of us who were there
watched it on television. I voted that morning. I knew
what had happened and I voted and I said to the poll worker
do you know that two planes hit the World Trade Center
and she said And wouldn't you know it happened on a day
when I can't go see it? and I said I think it's raining glass
and she said your probably right and then I went to work
because I didn't understand, and it wasn't until someone
came up to me on the street and said they hit the pentagon
and I realized that we were talking to each other and that
some barrier had fallen because this was so bad. Then
I understood. And then people started calling saying
are you all right, and the phones failed. You couldn't get
through. You know this. I know you know this. I know
you saw the pictures of the jumpers and I know you saw
the clouds of debris. I know you saw the listings
of the firefighters who died and the business people who
died and the janitors who died. But listen, this is important,
what you don't know is this. We handled it really well.
We came together. Every morning on the radio they told
us what they needed, and we took up collections at work
and bought gauze and peroxide and size thirteen boots.
We were all on volunteer lists so long we knew we would
never be called. Every night at eight on the dot we all
came out for candle light vigils, and we knew the route
of the firetrucks and we were there to cheer them on.
I just wanted you to know that we mourned. We talked
to each other. We helped each other. It was as bad
as you heard, but we were there for each other. We were.

Passing Food Up and Down the Table

At dinner after the conference, she says, no, she doesn't like her job,
she liked working at the auto plant better. Though she put the window
units in backwards, at first. Mid-size cars. Maybe some businessman
accelerating later through a mountain curve, sudden rain-scud, pressed
the button and got a st. vitus dance, open-close uncontrollable grimace.

She laughs.

Yeah, the auto plant. After that, food prep at the cannery. Now home health.
Like any job it's got its pros and cons. Like management trying to fire her.
The anti-war work, they can't stand it. But the flexibility is good. She
doesn't say a word about her clients, the going into an old person's
apartment, the sitting down by her on the crumpled bed, saying, *What do
you need? What can I get for you?* No, she says, she doesn't like the job at
all, but she gets to do exactly what they want to fire her for, the phone calls,
the press releases. *End death for corporate profit, end utility shutoffs. End
the fires.* In small closed rooms the kerosene fumes and blazes, fire eats up
the air, the furniture, a fuse of hair. She does what she needs to, daytime,
and writes up the work reports late at night. No, she's not worried about
losing the job, you can't worry about things like that, there's too much to do.

We are passing food up and down the table, twenty of us, szechuan bean curd,
noodles, and steamed salmon with rice. She says, *This fish gave its life for us,
the least we can do is eat every bit,* forking over the fretwork of bone,
and opening her mouth to taste the last shred of tattered flesh.

PAUL HOSTOVSKY

People in Deaf Houses

Here's the church and here's the steeple.
The deaf students have barricaded the door,
hot-wired the school buses, moved them
in front of the gates, and let the air out of the tires.
They've shut the campus down, and the police
can't do anything about it because they don't
know sign language. And neither does the president
of the college. And neither does the chairman of the board
of trustees, and neither do the trustees themselves.
The trustees can't be trusted with this college, this
church, this school, this blessed sacrament…

In the deaf world deaf is good. Deaf people marry
other deaf people, and live in deaf houses,
and do not throw deaf carpenters' telephone numbers
away, but give them to other deaf homeowners
looking for a good deaf carpenter, because deaf
is a good and trusted name all over the deaf world…

Here's the hospital and here's the urology unit.
Open the door and see all the doctors
with their deft fingers and expensive educations.
Here is one performing a vasectomy
on a deaf patient who has elected to have it
because he doesn't want any children.
And the surgeon has a slight accent, maybe
German. And the sign language interpreter
has a professional code of ethics,
and is signing what the surgeon is saying
but not what the interpreter is thinking
about German-speaking surgeons and vasectomies,
about Aryans and eugenicists and the forced
sterilizations of the congenitally deaf
in Europe only 40 years ago, about the protests
going on right now at Gallaudet, and about
cochlear implants being performed in this very
hospital, on deaf children who have not elected to have them…

Alexander Graham Bell invented the telephone.
He was a teacher of the deaf. He had a deaf mother,
and a deaf wife too, and he knew
that deaf people marry other deaf people
and live in deaf houses, and he deplored that fact.
He deplored deaf people. He urged Congress to act,
to prohibit deaf marriages, to reduce the risk
of more deaf babies. He wasn't a Hitler,
or an Eichmann exactly. He didn't advocate
killing the deaf. He loved the deaf. He taught the deaf.
He was only trying to eradicate the deaf
for their own good, for the good of the world…

In the deaf world deaf is good. In fact,
it's downright presidential.
Here's the church and here's the steeple.
Ring the doorbell, go ahead,

SUSAN LANG

Out the Window

No one should design a kitchen
without a window over the sink.
Imagine washing dishes

when you couldn't watch the clouds
break apart after an afternoon rain,
backlit so their centers glow

like swirling clouds in Tiepolo's
paintings, the edges shredding
into neighbors' trees, or like papers

you read about in the Sunday *Times*,
memos "tangled in the boughs"
after days of protests in the streets

of a city you've never visited.
You don't know if the kitchens
in that city have windows,

you aren't familiar with the buildings
that line the central square, or the sound
of the sirens police use

in that city. But you can imagine
the papers, imagine throwing
fistfuls of papers from the office

which does, indeed, have a window
looking out over the square;
you can feel the wind that stirs the papers

like leaves that have not yet pushed
into the revolution of a painted sky.

CHRISTOPHER HENNESSY

To The Murdered Larry King, Oxnard, California

Tuesday, Feb. 13, 2008, 15-year-old Larry King was shot in the head in his computer
classroom in Oxnard, Calif. He was later pronounced brain dead. This poem was
written on Feb. 15, 2008, as Larry's killer faced hate crime charges for allegedly
targeting the eighth-grader for wearing makeup, jewelry and high heels and telling
people he was gay.

You selected lilac
fingernail polish,
a touch of peach
blush, and deep
purple eyeliner
the day before
you were murdered.

I am making this up,
the make-up colors.
For all I know, you
wore makeup so little,
so rarely, no one noticed
but the boys afraid
of how their skin pricked,

their pricks tensed
when you cast
your eyes down
as you past them
in the halls.
In the news photo
you could be coy,

shy...or maybe
you know something —
your smirk worthy
of Mona Lisa,
but with your full lips
and eyes like saucers
full of sweet, spilt coffee.

Tell them to sing
"Long Time Gone"
at your funeral, Larry.
I know you prefer the trio —
Nothing against Mister Young
I can hear you say — but
we all need an elegy these days.

When you shot hoops,
I hope your earrings jangled.
caught the sunlight
and spun rays of color
as if from a prism.
I hope a pretty bracelet
warms your wrist.

Even though we are
a nation of little boys
with clenched fists,
you wanted to sing
The Star-Spangled
Banner at your little bro's
baseball games.

Your diabetic mamma
is asking the blank-faced
reporter, Who
will remind me
to take my shots? Who
is going to feed Jasmine?
The name you gave the stray

dog who would only come
for you. Did you prefer
the canary or cream petals?
'Poet's Jasmine' for the perfume?
Or Arabic for the tea?
Why can't I stop
wishing you'd shot first?

During the days
your gone mind hummed
in your living body —
its gifts waiting to be 'harvested'
(the heart, a tiny gourd,
the kidney, summer beans?) —

I would, if I could,
give your purgatory
this one memory:
losing yourself
in the black glisten
of anise licorice sticks
hooked and dangling
in Bubbling Springs,
(Snagging crawdads!
For real!) — and conjuring
a boy, his eyes wet, oil-black,
his skin scented with jasmine,
his voice whispering,
I wish I had your smile.

LOIS ROMA-DEELEY

A Still Small Voice

No river with wide arms. No dry place high
upon the trees. No trembling bit of asphalt
cracking under the sun; no trainers with a whip
and gun. Not the slight bright ring or angel wing
pinned to a blue lapel. Nothing in the giant
shadows cast onto the windows of a skyscraper.
No form or shape. No saint to bless by name.
Not on TV or beside the street preacher. Not
under blue awnings or inside rose tattoos. No
fires are left burning. No Elijah waiting in the
voting booth, breaking into a long speech. Just
this standing inside the here and now, the whistle
of   listen,   listen,   listen

PATRICIA SMITH

And Now the News: Tonight, The Soldiers

dropped their guns to dance. The sight
of spinning starlit men, their arms
around such waiting waists, alarmed
those paid to blare the sexy words
of war. And how did these hard men
decide on just this time to twirl
in bloodied dust, and how do we
explain the skin to skin, their hips
aligned, dramatic dips — was that
a kiss? Some rumba, others throw
a soundtrack down — they pound deep drums,
they twang imagined strings, they blow
notes blasted blue through sandy winds,
they dream a stout piano's weight.
They spark the dance — the bop and twist,
the tango, yes, the trot and stroll,
the slither, slow, unmanly grind
within a brother's brazen arms.
And so analysis begins.
The talking heads can't spit enough.
The cameras catch the swirling men,
their thrown-back heads and bended backs,
the rhythm of their rite, the ways
they steam. The toothy anchors chant
their numbers and their names, to shame
them into still. But still the music
blows, the soldiers pivot, swing,
unleash their languid limbs, caress.
They don't slow down to weep or stop
to grieve their new-gone guns. The public
bray begins, the *song of killers*
killing must resume!, but then
the mirthful moon illuminates
the ball, our boys in dip and glide
and woo. We see the dancers' dangling
eyes and oddly open sores,
shattered shoulders, earlobes gone,
the halves of heads, the limp, the drag
of not quite legs. Tonight they dropped

their guns, and snagged a nasty bass
to roughride home. You hear the stomp,
the weary wheeze and grunt, the ragged
nudge of notes on air? You see
the whirling soldiers spin, the love
they braved, and oh my god, that kiss?

KATHLEEN HELLEN

Anthem at Graduation: The HBCU

For James Weldon Johnson (1871–1938) and Jimi Hendrix (1942–1970)

We sing the Book of Numbers
Mums, gladiolas swelling in their ribboned dress

Vaudeville of rejoicing, each a Lazarus
A choir of black faces, staged

Not run away but faith rehearsed
in normal schools for coloreds
in run-down auditoriums

There is a prayer after despair
Be not afraid

NICOLE WALKER

Arizona State Road 89 before
the Turn-Off to Tuba City

If you didn't know better, you'd say the whole place
was nothing but a skin of dirt hanging loose over old

bones. And I don't know better. I drive across
the reservation in my 1999 VW, windows up to keep

out the dust as it flies fur across the capsule of the car.
I see a dead horse, lying flat as the reservation

dirt, lying as sunken and useless as the electricity-free,
running-water free outposts where the trailers rust.

The wind makes its home on the inside here. As does
the dust. As does the fur. I like to pretend, since I don't

know, late at night, that the sound the wind makes
is the sound of horses and I don't know whether the sound

is of horses galloping or the sound of horses, lying down
on the dirt without water as the earth takes the electricity

back out of them. As I drive and look at the dead horse
whose hair-losing ribs are as dumb as the red dirt walls

that keep the wind from going any other place (the wind
stays down here), I keep my windows up. I don't know

if, when a dog runs out in front of the car, I should stop.
The dogs run here, bones jutting, like the wind runs here

thin and constant. I stop to check on the dog. To confirm
his tags are missing To count his ribs. I walk him back,

a quarter mile to the gas station where the Navajo man from
the reservation has seen my kind before. I ask the man if he knows

who owns the dog. He laughs at me like he laughs at the flies, good-
naturedly and says, "He's your dog." I am a fool. I think he means,

You touch him, you buy him. Or, he's following *you,* isn't
he? But instead of shooing me and the dog out of there, he clicks

to the dog, who walks toward him like he knows him. The man
gives him a bowl of refrigerator cool water, and lifts his eyebrow

toward the door, toward the horse, toward the dirt that now rises
in a haze of electric wind. "He's your dog, but I'll take care of him."

I follow the direction of his eyebrow, and get out of the man's
way, hills pulsing now, back into my quiet, fur-free car.

CRYSTAL WILLIAMS

Night Bloom

~For Jade, after Hayden

It makes no sense to say *things will get better*
because you will not understand until they *are* better
& they may not get better soon. There is always pain
in the world & you have seen so much of it.
I do not know how to explain other than to say,
I am so sorry your mother has died, Girl,
that her mother has turned her back, that your father
is a rogue & you are having to do this grown-up work alone.
I would like to tell you to be patient
but understand that right now you might only know fear.
Listen, then. & know this: it is okay to be fearful.
If you cannot believe that things will soften,
trust that I believe for you.
You will not remember all of this pain.
But when Darkness insists you attend his party
you will know the trapdoors & gloomy corners of that house.
& you alone will be able to find the garden
where beautiful Cereus is opening her eyes in the pitch black.

SHIRLEY GEOK-LIN LIM

Learning to love America

because it has no pure products

because the Pacific Ocean sweeps along the coastline
because the water of the ocean is cold
and because land is better than ocean

because I say we rather than they

because I live in California
I have eaten fresh artichokes
and jacarandas bloom in April and May

because my senses have caught up with my body
my breath with the air it swallows
my hunger with my mouth

because I walk barefoot in my house

because I have nursed my son at my breast
because he is a strong American boy
because I have seen his eyes redden when he is asked who he is
because he answers I don't know

because to have a son is to have a country
because my son will bury me here
because countries are in our blood and we bleed them

because it is late and too late to change my mind
because it is time.

ROBERT PRINGLE

A 1969 Version of 'Soon'

Ronnie slept in a bottom dresser drawer
as we turned south from Brown County State Park.
The Natchez Trace Parkway just opened,
and we wanted to "ride the beautiful wound" the length
of Mississippi, to relatives in San Antonio.
We stopped at Cypress Inn. Ronnie, with a little
help, walked in like a toddler Ronnie Lott,
climbed his high chair, ready to order.

Near dark at a gas station, our stereotypes
came to life. What seemed to be the owner
filled the tank, stared at Ronnie, our Ohio plates,
walked back to his Dr. Pepper and his assistant . . .
no legs, rocking on a mechanic's creeper.
Both seemed like hyenas waiting for their pack.
We camped a few miles beyond at Tishomingo.
Fog grew, swept over us in sheets. The camp fire
held off visions of Klan and crosses.

Past Tupelo, with Elvis 'lonesome tonight',
The Trace asphalt glided through miles of grave
yard, each historical mound and marker either
Indian or Confederate dead . . . too early for flowering
bushes and trees . . . old shades of green and black.
Alone on the road, except for Witch Dance, Pigeon
Roost, and Kosciusko where main street dust blew
from the noses of horses, colored store fronts,
forced black residents to cover their faces.

Signs for Philadelphia and Meridian,
more frequently, names of politicians stamped
like Imperial seals over the landscape . . Ross Barnett
Reservoir, Bayou Pierre, . . . we wondered how far down
you had to be for Plaquemines Parish and Leander Perez.

We reached Natchez, not realizing The Pilgrimage
was on . . . thirty ante bellum mansions open for tour.
Driving down to the river, anxious for what remained
of Natchez-Under-The-Hill, we passed fading saloon signs,

Jesebel Night Club and The Blue Cat, . . . not much left
of what a Methodist minister called, "dirty as Hottentots"
and "The Worst Hell Hole on Earth." .
In the d1stance, The Delta Queen plodded upstream.
We imagined a number of stops, new passengers, its arrival
in Cincinnati where Ronald currently practices law.

PATRICIA SMITH

Rebuilding

A razored sky, unsure of what it yields,
arcs over flattened blocks, upturned faces,
muted shards of organ. Each day reveals
inane thoughts of dance. All fleeting traces
of the needled rain, the roar, the black wind
swirl in the obscene shimmer of new nails
hammered into treated wood. The thick-skinned
bring a song up from their feet, but it fails
to drown out the big useless drone of work,
the busy sounds of lifting what is damned.
Paint the rubble pretty, hues gone berserk
with dry hope. It seems we have been programmed
to set chaos upright, scrub at the stain,
build our homes on rivers, waltz in the rain.

ALLISON HEDGE COKE

America, I Sing Back

a tribute for Phil Young, my father Robert Hedge Coke, Whitman, and Hughes

America, I sing back. Sing back what sung you in.
Sing back the moment you cherished breath.
Sing you home into yourself and back to reason.

Oh, before America began to sing, I sung her to sleep,
held her cradleboard, wept her into day.
My song gave her creation, prepared her delivery,
held her severed cord beautifully beaded.

My song helped her stand, held her hand for first steps,
nourished her very being, fed her, placed her three sisters strong.
My song comforted her as she battled my reason
broke my long held footing sure, as any child might do.

Lo, as she pushed herself away, forced me to remove myself,
as I cried this country, my song grew roses in each tear's fall.

My blood-veined rivers, painted pipestone quarries
circled canyons, while she made herself maiden fine.

Oh, but here I am, here I am, here, I remain high on each and every peak,
carefully rumbling her great underbelly, prepared to pour forth singing —

and sing again I will, as I have always done.
Never silenced unless in the company of strangers, singing
the stoic face, polite repose, polite, while dancing deep inside, polite
Mother of her world. Sister of myself.

When my song sings aloud again. When I call her back to cradle.
Call her to peer into waters, to behold herself in dark and light,
day and night, call her to sing along, call her to mature, to envision —
Then, she will make herself over. My song will make it so.

When she grows far past her self-considered purpose,
I will sing her back, sing her back. I will sing. Oh, I will — I do.

America, I sing back. Sing back what sung you in.

AFAA M. WEAVER

The Picnic, an Homage To Civil Rights

We spread torn quilts and blankets,
mashing the grass under us until it was hard,
piled the baskets of steamed crabs
by the trees in columns that hid the trunk,
put our coolers of soda pop
on the edges to mark the encampment,
like gypsies settling in for revelry
in a forest in Romania or pioneers
blazing through the land of the Sioux,
the Apache, and the Arapaho, looking guardedly
over our perimeters for poachers
or the curious noses of fat women
ambling past on the backs of their shoes.
The sun crashed through the trees,
tumbling down and splattering in shadows
on the baseball diamond like mashed bananas.
We hunted for wild animals in the clumps
of forests, fried hot dogs until the odor
turned solid in our nostrils like wood.
We were in the park.

One uncle talked incessantly, because he knew
the universe; another was the griot
who stomped his foot in syncopation
to call the details from the base of his mind;
another was a cynic who doubted everything,
toasting everyone around with gin.
The patriarchal council mumbled on,
while the women took the evening to tune
their hearts to the slow air and buzzing flies,
to hold their hands out so angels could stand
in their palms and give dispensation,
as we played a rough game of softball
in the diamond with borrowed gloves,
singing Chuck Berry and Chubby Checker,
diving in long lines into the public pool,
throwing empty peanut shells to the lion,
buying cotton candy in the aviary
of the old mansion, laughing at monkeys,
running open-mouthed and full in the heat

until our smell was pungent and natural,
while the sun made our fathers and uncles
fall down in naps on their wives' laps, and
we frolicked like wealthy children on an English estate,
as reluctant laws and bloodied heads
tacked God's theses on wooden doors,
guaranteed the canopy of the firmament above us.

ALLISON JOSEPH

Xenophilia

Sing to me a language I don't speak
with vowels swirling round my ears like silk,
fingertips lifting candied morsels to my mouth,

tidbits freed from multicolored tins, their labels
printed in the ancient hieroglyphs of pre-war
factories, machines like monarchs.

Sing to me of settlements, of dust you cannot
wipe from your family name, of carousels
and caravans, tiny stringed instruments in velvet

cases packed away in steamer trunks stuffed
with sepia photos adamant in their frames.
Whisper secrets only your people know,

untranslatable lullabies lilting me into sleep
deeper than rivers by towns now wiped
off any map, a disappeared cartography.

I need to hear click songs and umlauts,
trilled r's and double "l"s, surnames
restored to multisyllabic glory from Ellis

Island simplifications. Share with me
your history's hope chest — bibles and brooches,
parchment-thin letters with faded fountain scrawls,

recite epic poems until I swoon, shuddering
under blankets woven by women blackshouldered
beneath mantillas of gypsy lace, generations

of widows intimate with the world's grace
— those tender of graves, singers of hymns,
prayer beads worried between leather palms.

LUIS H. FRANCIA

#7: Prayer for Peace

May a bird kill a cannon
and a baby destroy a gun
May buildings banish missiles
and children stop tanks
May a mother's love bury bombs
and hand grenades
May palm trees and olive groves
overwhelm planes with their
beauty and bounty
May the rivers and the earth repel
all things that stain and sully them
May blood spilled flow back into the
veins of the innocent dead
May families rise up out of the ashes
to break bread once more
May love curl around the barren hearts of men
May the flowers of imagination bloom in their minds
May our wars be only of words, never of swords
May the gods we pray to be
without history, without names
without nations, without creeds
without religion
May I love you in laughter and grace all the
Days without end

Occupation

Occupy Wall Street Occupy Dream Street Occupy the Mississippi River Occupy Rocky Mountains Occupy Jet Stream Occupy Ozone Layer Occupy Business Ethics Occupy Temple Emmanuel Occupy Saint Patricks Occupy Bank of America Occupy America Occupy Smiles Occupy Baseball Occupy Florida Occupy Texas Occupy Wonders of the Universe Occupy Deep Hearts Occupy Dawn's Early Light Occupy God Bless America Occupy This Land Is My Land Occupy Song of Myself Occupy Buddha's Eye Occupy the Bright Green Light Across the Bay

Occupy the small spaces in our hearts. Dream of possibilities and wake up with them done. Occupy the hopes that deserve those dreams. Sleep with the thoughts of all the kids who learn to spell their names. Occupy the sky and the stars that memorize their names. Eat with fingers that taste possibilities. Praise the teachers who speak those names. Occupy the small spaces in our hearts as wide as the sky. That's what a new world looks like. Now that all of us are awake, it's time to dream.

Contributor's Notes

Sherman Alexie is a writer, poet, filmmaker, and occasional comedian. Much of his writing draws on his experiences as a Native American. Two of Alexie's best known works are *The Lone Ranger and Tonto Fistfight in Heaven* and *Smoke Signals*, a film. *The Absolutely True Diary of a Part-Time Indian*, an autobiographical young adult novel, won a National Book Award. His latest book is *War Dances*.

Indran J. Amirthanayagam's latest book is *The Splintered Face: Tsunami Poems*. Proceeds from that book are donated towards tsunami relief.

Rane Arroyo was an American poet, playwright, and scholar of Puerto Rican descent who wrote numerous books and received many literary awards. He was a professor of English and Creative Writing at the University of Toledo in Ohio. Some of his most recent books of poetry include *Same-Sex Séances*, *The Buried Sea: New & Selected Poems*, and *The Sky's Weight*. He passed away in 2010.

His life partner Glenn Sheldon writes: "Rane Arroyo is a human of many poetic talents (here I prefer the literary present tense, as he died an untimely death on May 7, 2010, at the age of 55). Many, by that age (particularly academics), have accomplished all they are going to accomplish. One of the many tragedies here is that is not Rane. He leaves behind a wealth of unpublished poems, plays, versions of memoirs (and even a novel, I suspect). And he would have continued to produce many more brilliant works. Importantly, Rane resented when people would write about him and exclude that he is an openly gay, Puerto Rican poet. In an era that has an impulse to be post-label, Arroyo believes that labels can give courage, strength and the message that — in spite of your background (whatever it may be) — you can make it, too.

As Rane's life partner for 28 years (and a few days), I can only speculate about his impulse(s) for this poem. He supported Obama, but he also distrusted that Obama could topple the DC machine of (white) greed, corruption and power. Born in 1954, Rane would have been 18 when Ms. Chisholm became this nation's first major-party African American candidate for president. I think this poem is about not forgetting that Obama won the White House, but he is not a pioneer in the race for it — Ms. Chisholm was. In addition to voting for minimum wage, I think Rane admired her support base that was ethnically diverse (he believed in inclusivity, ultimately, which is also a contributing factor for Obama's success). And Rane included women and their struggles as "second-class citizens," and Ms. Chisholm certainly had the support of NOW. (Oh how Rane cringed when a female student in his class would say I believe in equal rights for women, but I don't like to be called a "feminist"!). Even now in the face of disappointing gay rights advances, I hear the line from this poem: "It's hard work to be safe / to own the future that's ours to bewitch." At his last public poetry reading, he began his poem, "In Defense of Marriage," a poem about gay rights, with a more didactic paraphrase of those poetic lines: 'I am NOT a second-class citizen.'"

David Baker's most recent book of poems is *Never-Ending Birds*. He resides in Granville, Ohio, where he serves as poetry editor of *The Kenyon Review*. He teaches at Denison University and in the M.F.A. program for writers at Warren Wilson College.

Baker writes: "Poetry as an art is resistance. That's part of its purpose and also its beauty. It resists even as it absorbs the languages of coercion and reduction — the languages of advertising and politics, for instance, all the other dumbed-down languages that seek to take our power rather than, like poetry, to give us power. Poetry gives us the power of the imagination, its freedoms and discoveries.

"The Spring Ephemerals" is about resistance. The two people in the poem want to resist the overwhelming power of business and "development," the spreading human stain that erases the natural world, scrapes it away, and replaces it with the artificial and the unnatural. They want to save a few fragile flowers. They want to name the names of things. They want to make a map to remember, just as poetry maps out a form of memory.

This is also a love poem. For nature. For the scarred and adored body of the world. For the scarred and adored body of the lover. For each poem's capability to say, to name, to remember, and thus to save, at least for a little while."

Marvin Bell's current books are *Mars Being Red* and *7 Poets, 4 Days, 1 Book* — co-authored by poets from five countries. Forthcoming books include: *Vertigo: The Living Dead Man Poems*; *Whiteout*, a collaboration with the photographer Nathan Lyons, from Lodima; and a children's picture book, from Candlewick Press, based on "A Primer about the Flag." A song cycle, "The Animals," commissioned by the composer David Gompper, premiered in 2009. Long on the faculty of the Iowa Writers' Workshop, and Iowa's first Poet Laureate, he teaches now for the brief-residency MFA based in Oregon at Pacific University and lives in Iowa City and Port Townsend, Washington.

Bell writes: "In early 1998 I was asked by Burns Weston, the University of Iowa Professor of Law who in 1999 would spearhead the founding of The University of Iowa Center for Human Rights, to write a poem for the fiftieth anniversary of the adoption, on December 10, 1948, of the Universal Declaration of Human Rights. I wrote and revised the poem in February and March of 1998. The poem then appeared in The Iowa Review, in a book edited by Professor Weston, and later in a State Department booklet on human rights. There may also exist a broadside of it. I confess I have lost track. I think of the poem as anyone's words. It need not carry my byline.

I thought to make the poem generally applicable to matters of rights and justice. I couldn't not feel that a few questions bearing a hint of accusation might be to the point, and so I sandwiched them in between passages of imagery from the natural world. Hence, the first and last stanzas. When I arrived at stanza three, I switched the pronouns so that each line of those two stanzas apply to both men and women.

I try always to say yes to such assignments. Poetry, like philosophy, is a survival skill, but need not be an escape. An art form, however self-contained, is also a manifestation of matters beyond aesthetics. As for commissions to produce a poem for an occasion, I tend to favor the poem that is about the occasion for an event rather than about the event itself. That does not apply, of course, to the news, which I prefer to meet head-on."

Dan Bellm is a poet and translator living in San Francisco. His third book of poetry, *Practice*, won a California Book Award and was named one of the year's top ten poetry books by the *Virginia Quarterly Review*. He teaches Spanish to English Literary Translation online for New York University.

Bellm writes: "In its final chapters, the Book of Exodus contains incredibly elaborate building specs for the ritual paraphernalia — the ark of the covenant, the moveable sanctuary — that the Israelites were commanded to schlep for forty years of nomadic wandering from slavery in Egypt to the Promised Land. I am fascinated by the apparent contradiction between this highly un-portable accumulation of stuff and the essentially abstract nature of Jewish belief. We don't make idols or represent the divine in any way, because it can't be seen; the four-letter name of God can't even be pronounced. What were we carrying? Is a spiritual calling, a command to transform from a nation of slaves to a free people, a call to justice, also a burden? I began this poem by thinking about weight and emptiness, and the strange root relationship between the Hebrew words for "glory" and "heaviness," kavod and kaved."

Patrick Bizzaro has published eight books and chapbooks of poetry, two critical studies of Fred Chappell's poetry and fiction, a book on the pedagogy of academic creative writing, some textbooks, and a couple hundred poems in magazines. He lives quite happily with Resa Crane and their three-year-old son, Antonio, in Indiana, PA. In his last year at ECU, he received the "Outstanding Professor" award from the ECU Department of Disability Support Services, the ninth award for teaching he has received during his career. He is a Professor of English at IUP, teaching in the doctoral program in C&T and in the undergraduate writing program.

Bizarro writes: "After marrying my wife, Resa, who is Cherokee and Meherrin, and we decided to have a baby together, Antonio, I realized that Native American intermarriage over the years has resulted in fewer "pure Native Americans," so much so that it seems those Native Americans who remain will become so small in number they will have limited political sovereignty. This poem is my statement of honor to my wife and child for respecting the ways they are tied to and understanding the importance of difference on this planet."

Ralph Black is the author of a collection of poems, *Turning over the Earth*.

Lindsey Brown lives in New York. This is her first poetry publication.

Claudia Carlson is an award-winning graphic designer. Her first book of poetry, *The Elephant House*, was published by Marsh Hawk Press in 2007. She co-edited, with Jeanne Marie Beaumont, *The Poets' Grimm: 20th Century Poems from Grimm Fairy Tales*, an anthology of modern fairy tale poems. She had a one woman portrait show in at the Cornelia Street Café in New York City in 2011. See www.claudiagraphics.com for her visual work and claudiacarlson.blogspot. com. She lives in Manhattan with her husband, lyricist Jim Racheff.

Carlson writes: "When I was a girl visiting my family in Flatbush, Brooklyn, my grandmother would treat me to trips into Manhattan to see museums and musicals. As we walked from lunch at Lord & Taylors to a matinee on Broadway, I enjoyed the pastel artwork on the concrete sidewalks. They were mostly biblical scenes copied from Renaissance paintings.

When I moved to the Upper West Side after college, I once again found art under my feet. But in the years since I had been a girl, the replications of angels and saints had changed into something more interesting. I soon recognized the work of one artist, Hani Shihada. He draws like a student of Michaelangelo but creates portraits based in our times: from the young Michael Jackson to Hilary Clinton, the other Madonna to Ted Kennedy and even Sponge Bob got his square moment. Warm dry weather brings Hani back to the New York public as a street artist, often in my neighborhood.

His story is moving. He told me he grew up in a country where Israel was the enemy and only his interest in art kept him from devoting himself to destruction. He went to Italy and learned to paint. He came to America and learned to accept, befriend, and honor people of every race, religion, and class.

I love watching him work. He scrapes away the gum, covers skid marks, and then with his bag of pastels, he creates his moving, mutable portraits. He answers questions with a calm smile. I've noticed it takes about two years for these paintings to fully fade away. In this way we recognize our heroes and hopes even as our own feet erase them through our daily journeys."

Sarah Cedeño was born and raised in Brockport, NY, where she teaches English composition and the occasional writing workshop at the College at Brockport. Having taken a hiatus from writing to digest her diagnosis with MS, marry her husband, Cory, and have her son, John (in that order), she is happy to be writing again.

Cedeño writes: "This poem began as a fragment of a creative nonfiction piece I was working on, but branched off in another direction entirely. What started as personal reflection on the diagnosis literally "walked" itself into public. There is something about the community that surrounds a disease (the professional community, the fundraising community, the family community) that feels oddly cheerful (and inspiring) to me. What I hope this poem captured was the effort of these communities that, while masking the same sadness and frustration that I have with illness, push their emotion towards productive and resonant action when someone with the disease might not be able to."

Kevin Clark is the author of *Self-Portrait with Expletives, In the Evening of No Warning*, and a poetry writing textbook *The Mind's Eye: A Guide to Writing Poetry*
   Clark writes: "'Elizabeth at Seabrook' is based on a true story. My wife was a protester at the site of the Seabrook (New Hampshire) nuclear power plant before it was built. Devoted to non-violent action, she and hundreds of others were arrested and placed in an armory. When the peaceful prisoners refused to plead guilty after days of incarceration, the National Guard threatened to split the men from the women. A Quaker woman among the protesters came up with the plan as described in the poem and announced it to the National Guard. Soon afterward the prisoners were released."

Allison Hedge Coke is an American Book Award-winning American/Canadian poet of mixed Wendat, Huron, Metis, Tsalagi, Creek, French Canadian, Portuguese, Irish, Scot, and English ancestry. Her books include *Blood Run and Rock, Ghost*, and *Willow Deer: A Story of Survival*.

Martha Collins is the author of the book-length poem *Blue Front*, which won an Anisfield-Wolf Award and was chosen as one of the New York Public Library's 2006 "25 Books to Remember." She has also published four earlier collections of poems, two collections of co-translations of Vietnamese poetry, and two chapbooks. Editor-at-large for *FIELD* magazine, she served as Distinguished Visiting Writer at Cornell University.
   Collins writes: "'Birmingham" marks the beginning of a trip — and also the beginning of a book-length project that changed the direction of my work and my life.
   In 2000, following the itinerary of a friend who'd taken the trip a year before, I drove to Alabama to visit civil rights sites and museums. Birmingham was the first stop, and the poem reflects notes I took while I was there: first at the 16th Street Baptist Church, then at the Birmingham Civil Rights Institute across the street. By the time I wrote the poem two years later, I'd also read Diane McWhorter's *Carry Me Home: Birmingham, Alabama: The Climactic Battle of the Civil Rights Revolution.*
   I read McWhorter's book because it explored her father's possible involvement in Klan-related reactions to the civil rights movement, and I was now exploring a lynching that my father witnessed as a five-year-old in Cairo, Illinois. My exploration in fact came about because of the Alabama journey. When I told a New York friend about the trip, she told me about an exhibit of lynching postcards at the New York Historical Society. In the exhibit, I discovered a series of postcards from a lynching in Cairo and realized, for the first time, that the hanging my father told me he'd seen as a kid was in fact a brutal lynching. That was the beginning of my exploration of the event, which resulted in the book-length poem Blue Front."

Sean Thomas Dougherty is a self described "underground sound." He is the author or editor of eleven books including *Sasha Sings the Laundry on the Line*, the novella *The Blue City*, and *Broken Hallelujahs*. He is the recipient of two Pennsylvania Council for the Arts Fellowships in poetry and a Fulbright Lectureship to Macedonia. He lives in Erie, Pa.

Dougherty writes: "My poem 'After the Election' was written one spring day after a hard rain when it seemed as if something miraculous had happened, that everything had turned to joy, as everyone, it seemed, in my small city along lake Erie, was full of the most ethereal light, and I imagined, in a moment that some great election had occurred, that a president had been elected who would "turn the jails into print shops." This was during the darkest of the Bush years when I felt the weight of the government's fascist attitudes and policies and felt like a foreigner and outcast in my own nation. This poem was an attempt to remake the world, to use my words to imagine something beyond the present as possible. I learned this from Neruda, not to let the great THEM take the world from us, to imagine the possible means that it remains possible, part of the struggle for human justice, and how it must involve Joy. And it begins in language, and how we see ourselves, and how we shape "the words no one has yet to define." And if we can do that, if you who are reading can do this, can imagine a place where the oppression has been resisted and replaced, well then together we can cross arms, we can begin together to make that world, the two of us, then maybe three of us, then four of us, and onward until enough of us join hands."

Denise Duhamel's most recent poetry titles are *Ka-Ching!*; *Two and Two*; *Mille et un Sentiments*; *Queen for a Day: Selected and New Poems*; and *The Star-Spangled Banner*. A bilingual edition of her poems, *Afortunada de mí* (*Lucky Me*), translated into Spanish by Dagmar Buchholz and David Gonzalez, was released with Bartleby Editores (Madrid) in 2008. A recipient of a National Endowment for the Arts fellowship, she is an associate professor at Florida International University in Miami.

Duhamel writes: "I wrote "David Lemieux" in 1986, after hearing that my junior high school boyfriend had died of AIDS. This was in the early years of the epidemic when there was a lot of misinformation and discrimination against those with AIDS."

Cheryl Dumesnil is the author of *In Praise of Falling*, editor of *Hitched! Wedding Stories from San Francisco City Hall*, and co-editor, with Kim Addonizio, of *Dorothy Parker's Elbow: Tattoos on Writers, Writers on Tattoos*. She lives in the San Francisco Bay Area with her wife and their two sons.

Dumesnil writes: "I wrote "Hard Labor" when I was in my mid-twenties, at a time when I was learning to shape my life based on what I valued rather than on what I thought others wanted me to value. Back then, walking an unpopular path felt difficult in many ways, but the rewards were undeniable. This poem celebrates both the sense of community that we can create in the midst of strug-gle and the rich, fulfilling lives we can build when we make decisions that reso-nate well with our true selves."

Martín Espada is the author of several collections of poetry including: *The Trouble Ball: Poems*; *The Republic of Poetry*, which was a finalist for the Pulitzer Prize in Poetry, and *Alabanza: New and Selected Poems* (1982-2002), which received the Paterson Award for Sustained Literary Achievement and was named an American Library Association Notable Book of the year.

Blas Falconer is the author of *A Question of Gravity and Light* and a co-editor of *Mentor and Muse: Essays from Poets to Poets*. He teaches at Austin Peay State University, where he coordinates creative writing and acts as poetry editor of *Zone 3: A Literary Journal.*

Falconer writes: "My partner and I live in a house that stands on a large hill facing downtown Nashville. The speaker in the poem is looking out over the city to consider those who have lived and died there, including soldiers in the Civil War battle and those who participated in sit-ins at the Woolworth and McLellan lunch counters. Although the area of town is becoming gentrified, and the old signs of the past are fading, the speaker and his partner stay put in their old home. They help each other in simple ways to build a life together, to love one another, and in doing so, they stand in protest against whatever might challenge their union, whether that be bigotry or some other unidentified challenge."

Luis H. Francia is the author of several books. His poetry collections include *Museum of Absences* and *The Arctic Archipelago and Other Poems*. *The Beauty of Ghosts* was published in 2010, as well as *A History of the Philippines: From Indios Bravos to Filipinos*. He edited *White Ocean: An Anthology of Twentieth Century Philippine Literature in English*. He teaches Philippine-American Literature at Hunter College and Tagalog Language and Culture at New York University.

Francia writes: "September 11, 2001 was very much on my mind when I put together the poems that make up Museum of Absences (2004), in which "#7: Prayer for Peace" is included. Bush's so-called Global War on Terror had led to the senseless war on Iraq, hence the reference in the poem to palm trees and olive groves. I also remembered how in 1986 Filipinos confronted non-violently the armed might of the tyrannical Marcos regime. In the end, the dictator and his wife fled the country. My friends and I in New York were delirious with joy, that our countrymen had succeeded with nothing but prayers, food, and above all with love. No dream is impossible, after all."

M Gioia is the spawn of a hermetic genius and a reformed rapscallion. She made her stage debut tap-dancing across the OBGYN floor of Balboa hospital and since then has been a cute baby, an ugly child, an awkward pre-adolescent, a sul-len teenager, and a jaded twenty-something. She is now waiting patiently for the next cliché. At the age of eighteen she went into indentured servitude as a linguist and came out four years later a meteorologist. Sometimes she writes things. Sometimes she tries to publish them. Sometimes she watches one episode of a television show and then spends all night on Megavideo watching the entire series and waiting out the 72-minute limit between episodes. She likes things that are pretty. She has a dog who runs like a zombie and a boyfriend who calls her Marmalade Dingy Parfait, Esquire. Her favorite symbol is the interrobang and her favorite shape is the star.

Of "Rookery Mockery," Gioia writes: "The story of the gay penguins really got to me. I thought it was so lovely that there were two male penguins who partnered and raised a chick together, and I actually got kind of emotional when I read that the zookeepers had introduced a female penguin and one of the males had gone off with her. At first I wanted to sit that male penguin down and have a talk about heteronormativity, but then I realized I was just upset that he was making bisexuals look bad. Resist those labels, little penguin; you don't have to be my representative!

This began as a series of haiku and expanded outward. Usually I find that haiku forces me to write only the exactly correct word, but in this case the poem resisted containment. I have too many words to write about this topic; who knew?"

Renny Golden, an activist, poet, and academic, currently lives in Albuquerque, NM, where she teaches at the University of New Mexico. She is Professor Emerita at Northeastern Illinois University, where she received the Faculty Excellence Award four times and the Womens Studies Social Justice Award in 2005, which has been named the Renny Golden Award. She was a finalist for the C. Wright Award for her book *War on Families: Imprisoned Mothers and the Families They Leave Behind.* Her poetry collection *Hour of the Furnaces* was nominated for the National Book Award, and her most recent book of poetry, *Blood Desert: Witnesses, 1820-1880*, was published in 2010.

Rigoberto González is the author of two poetry books, *So Often Goes the Pitcher Until It Breaks*, a National Poetry Series selection, and *Other Fugitives and Other Strangers*; two bilingual children's books: *Soledad Sigh-Sighs/Soledad Suspiros* and *Antonio's Card/La tarjeta de Antonio*; the novel *Crossing Vines*; the story collection *Men without Bliss*; and a memoir, *Butterfly Boy.*

González writes: "I grew up Mexican Catholic, and I believed that there was a unique poetry in listening to Mass in Spanish and in praying with the vocabulary of my native tongue. I longed for these experiences and romanticized the memory of them as soon as I moved to the U.S., where my family stopped going to church because these sterile, blank buildings were nothing like the colonial architectures of Mexico.

I was in for another rude awakening when I went to college and came across the terror of the sidewalk preacher — fanatic Christians that emptied their faith of intimacy and respect when they stood in public areas and cast hell-fire accusations at us as we walked to our classes. I was shocked that freedom of speech meant freedom to hate-speech.

As an immigrant college student I wanted to come to terms with these contradictions: hatred in the name of religion, ignorance in a place of learning, the personal shifting to the political. So I read books and found no answers, just marvelous questions that helped me decide to become a writer who could reclaim some of that mystery and beauty I remembered as a child.

As for the sidewalk preacher with his useless language and dead soul...well, I take comfort in that I will always have my Mexico."

Brent Goodman has worked as a teacher, musician, technical writer, and web designer. He is the author of *The Brother Swimming Beneath Me, Wrong Horoscope*, and *Trees Are the Slowest Rivers*. He lives in northern Wisconsin with his partner and three cats, where he works as a creative professional.

Barbara Hamby's most recent book of poems is *All-Night Lingo Tango*. She was born in New Orleans and raised in Hawai'i. She now lives in Tallahassee, Florida where she teaches creative writing in the English Department at Florida State University. Most recently her book of stories, *Lester Higata's 20th Century*, won the Iowa Short Fiction Prize/John Simmons Award. She also published *Seriously Funny*, an anthology of poetry that she co-edited with her husband David Kirby.

Sam Hamill is the author of fifteen volumes of original poetry, including *Almost Paradise: Selected Poems and Translations* and *Measured by Stone*. He has also published more than two dozen volumes of poetry translated from classical Chinese, Japanese, Greek, Latin, and Estonian, as well as four volumes of essays on the practice of poetry, notably *A Poet's Work and Avocations: On Poets and Poetry*. He is Founding Editor of Copper Canyon Press where he served as Editor for thirty-two years. He lives in Anacortes, Washington.

Hamill writes: "'True Peace' was inspired by a journey through Vietnam with The Joiner Center for the Study of War and Social Consequences, and sitting in while Nguyen Ba Chung and Kevin Bowen interviewed 1st, 2nd, and 3rd generation victims of Agent Orange. Thich Quang Dúc was one of Thich Nhat Hanh's teachers, and we visited his native temple in Hue. I was often asked by Vietnamese writers to tell how I became radicalized against war while serving in the Marine Corps and how I came to found Poets Against War. The poem was born in a single draft several months later, as I remembered my experiences in Okinawa, a country still overrun by U.S. military bases."

Tom Healy was raised on a farm in Mount Vision, New York. He earned a BA in philosophy from Harvard University and an MFA in creative writing from Columbia University. His first collection of poetry, *What the Right Hand Knows*, was a finalist for the L.A. Times Book Award and the Lambda Literary Award in Poetry.

Kathleen Hellen has won the *Washington Square Review*, James Still and Thomas Merton poetry prizes, as well as individual artist grants from the state of Maryland and the city of Baltimore. Her chapbook *The Girl Who Loved Mothra* is forthcoming from Finishing Line Press. She is a contributing editor for the *Baltimore Review*.

Hellen writes: "The old auditorium on the Baltimore campus had been named after James Weldon Johnson, whose anthem we were singing. "Sing a song full of the faith that the dark past has taught us," the words tell us. It was October. The stage boasted yellow mums and purple gladiolas. I had on the required regalia — cap and gown, symbol of my own passage into the great discourse of humanity. Although the Civil Rights Movement had ended many years before I entered college, the anthems that had scored those turbulent years still resounded in my memory: "We Shall Overcome" and "The Times They Are a-Changin." Hendrix's electric distortions of "The Star-Spangled Banner" still served as an anthem against the abuses of power. As we continued with "Lift Every Voice and Sing," often called "The Negro National Anthem," the raw emotions surfaced. The whole history of civil rights distilled in that moment with the sense of how different it had been for these young students sitting here that day. And yet how little things had changed. Most were first-generation college students and many ill-prepared for the rigorous coursework they faced; many were from single-parent homes, some were parents themselves. Many were poor. Perhaps one in every 10 had at least one incarcerated family member. Perhaps six out of every 10 knew someone battling substance abuse. Almost everyone knew somebody who'd been shot. When you teach at Coppin State University where the graduation rate is at 19 percent, among the lowest in the nation, every Fall convocation, every new semester, is cause for rejoicing. I wrote "Anthem at Graduation" as a praise song for my students at this historically black university. Their faith and courage sustain me."

Christopher Hennessy is the editor of *Outside the Lines: Talking with Contemporary Gay Poets*.

Hennessy writes: "When gay college student Matthew Shepard was brutally murdered in Wyoming in 1998, the world responded with grief, anger — -and protests from across the country to end gay-bias crimes. A decade later, another senseless hate crime would shock with similar force. The morning of Feb. 12, 2008, eighth grader Lawrence (Larry) King was in his school's computer room in Oxnard, Calif., when classmate Brandon McInerney shot him in the head, according to police. Larry had been bullied by students for being openly gay. Days before he had asked McInerney to be his Valentine in front of McInerney's friends. Larry was taken off life support and died on Valentine's Day.

I found in the news accounts of King's murder details of a life of struggle but, too, an inspiring life of a loving young boy who had sought to be true to himself. Struggling against a deep sadness, I turned to poetry. I hoped to show the richness of Larry's life and to mourn a society that had created another young man so bereft of empathy and so full of hate. Shortly after I wrote the poem and posted it online, a ninth-grader at high school near Larry's wrote me an email. She told me she'd taken part in a peace walk at her school in memory of Larry and that she'd found my poem read it at the event. Her words renewed my faith in young people…and in the power of poetry. Perhaps this can give us hope that one day love — and poetry — will rise up and stake its claim for good.

Postscript: In 2008, almost 10,000 people were the victims of hate crimes, according to the FBI. In October of 2009 President Obama signed into law the groundbreaking Matthew Shepard and James Byrd, Jr., Hate Crimes Prevention Act.

William Heyen is Professor of English/Poet in Residence Emeritus at SUNY Brockport, his undergraduate alma mater. A former Senior Fulbright Lecturer in American Literature in Germany, he has won NEA, Guggenheim, American Academy & Institute of Arts & Letters, and other fellowships and awards. He is the editor of *American Poets in 1976, The Generation of 2000: Contemporary American Poets*, and *September 11, 2001: American Writers Respond*. His books include *Pig Notes & Dumb Music: Prose on Poetry* and *Crazy Horse in Stillness; Shoah Train: Poems*, a Finalist for the National Book Award, and *The Confessions of Doc Williams: Poems* from Etruscan Press. Carnegie-Mellon University Press has published his first book, *Depth of Field*, in its Classic Contemporaries Series.

Heyen writes: "I don't even remember now what kind of tree it was, but years ago I was walking on the campus at the University of Georgia in Athens when I came to it where a road divided to accommodate it. A plaque said that the tree had been willed to itself, that it belonged to itself forever.

Traffic had to adjust to the tree, not vice-versa. It was a free entity. This was a hopeful discovery for me during a time when I was giving readings that focused on Bill McKibben's *The End of Nature* and when my ecology poems that became the book *Pterodactyl Rose* were coming into being. Because of that tree in Georgia, because of someone's gift of giving that tree to itself, I in turn received the gift of "Emancipation Proclamation.""

Scott Hightower is the author of *Part of the Bargain*, winner of the Hayden Carruth Award for New and Emerging Poets, as well as *Tin Can Tourist*, and *Natural Trouble*. His translations of poems from the Spanish have garnered Hightower a Willis Barnstone Translation Prize.

Hightower writes: "Virgil (who witnessed the effects of Caesar's land reform policies) and W.H. Auden (who left war-torn Europe to live on St. Marks Street in the east village of New York City) are two poets I think of who elected to in some way write about and to what was going on in their contemporary world. Writing overtly political poetry is very, very difficult. Diatribe and empathy for injustice are two different things. And the line in writing makes all the difference between being an insightful writer and being an insufferable writer. Injustice can be linked easily to despair or to hope. One comes back to the old dialectic of writing realistically or idealistically. Oscar Wilde (in the Preface of *Dorian Gray*) wrote: "There is no such thing as a moral or an immoral book. Books are well written, or badly written. That is all. The nineteenth century dislike of realism is the rage of Caliban seeing his own face in a glass. The nineteenth century dislike of romanticism is the rage of Caliban not seeing his own face in a glass." People who cannot imagine a more just world will never live in one."

Matthew Hittinger is the author of the chapbooks *Pear Slip*, winner of the Spire 2006 Chapbook Award, *Narcissus Resists*, and *Platos de Sal*. He lives and works in New York City.

Paul Hostovsky is the author of *Bending the Notes* and *Dear Truth*. He makes his living as an interpreter at the Massachusetts Commission of the Deaf and Hard of Hearing where he specializes in working with the deaf-blind.

Hostovsky writes: "Deaf President Now was a student-led protest in 1988 at Gallaudet University, the only liberal arts college for the deaf in the world. The board of trustees had chosen a hearing candidate (with no sign language skills or knowledge of deaf education) over several qualified deaf applicants for the position of president of the university. The chairman of the board, by way of explanation, is reported to have said, "Deaf people are not yet ready to function in the hearing world." About 7 years before that, I took my first sign language class. About 40 years before that, the Nazis were systematically sterilizing deaf people all over Europe. About 40 years before that, A.G. Bell was advocating for a law that would prevent deaf people from marrying other deaf people. And today, audiologists all over the world are telling parents of deaf infants that an invasive procedure called a cochlear implant will go a long way toward making their deaf children function better in the hearing world. And today, when I happen to see two deaf people signing in public — on the train, say, or in a restaurant — I still get that little catch in my throat, that devastating sweet gasp that you sometimes feel in the presence of gorgeous music, famous people, or angels."

Langston Hughes (February 1, 1902 – May 22, 1967) was a major American Poet from the Harlem Renaissance to the Civil Rights Movement of the 1950s and 1960s.

Colette Inez resides in Manhattan with husband Saul Stadtmauer, a freelance writer and journalist. Her newest collection, *Horseplay*, will be published by Word Press.

Charles Jensen is the author of *The First Risk*, which was a finalist for the Lambda Literary Award. His previous chapbooks include *Living Things* and *The Strange Case of Maribel Dixon*. He is a past recipient of an Artist's Project Grant from the Arizona Commission on the Arts. He is the founding editor of the online poetry magazine *LOCUSPOINT*, which explores creative work on a city-by-city basis, and serves as the poetry editor for Lethe Press.

Jensen writes: "For several weeks, I pored over any remains of the Matthew Shepard murder I could locate from the safe space of my office. I Googled magazine articles, courtroom transcripts, and obituaries. I scrolled through endless websites where Matthew's face in the same black and white photo stared out at me, unchanged, ageless. I went back to that year and recalled what it meant for me to watch his death unfold on television screens and newspaper headlines. I remembered the jarring juxtaposition of his full name, Matthew, as spoken by journalists, colliding with the name by which he was intimately known, Matt.

At the thumbnail level, the event is just data. There was a boy and a body and a field, and it was October, and I was twenty-one. The detail was fogging up in our cultural mirror and we could no longer see the event, or ourselves in it. I began to write about Matthew because people were starting to forget him. Worse, hate crimes against gays, lesbians, and transgendered people were continuing with startling frequency. I remembered how Matthew's death seemed to make everyone in the United States stop for a moment and universally decry the actions of the two men who took his life. I thought for a while that perhaps this meant hetereosexual America would no longer tolerate this kind of violence. But I was wrong, and more and more people were beaten or killed, and still I grew older while Matthew did not.

That I have to explain to people who Matthew was when I read from this work angers me. That my book had to include a historical note about the events that transpired that night in October angers me. I do not find this kind of ignorance among gay audiences; it is only the straight people who have moved away from their remembering. And it is for that reason these poems exist. It is because straight people can forget, that they are able to forget, that they have allowed themselves to forget that these poems exist."

Rodney Jones, an Alabama native, is a professor of English at Southern Illinois University Carbondale. He was a Pulitzer Prize finalist for *Elegy for the Southern Drawl*, a National Book Critics Circle Award winner for *Transparent Gestures* and a Kingsley Tufts Poetry Award winner for his new and selected collection *Salvation Blues*.

Allison Joseph is the author of five full-length collections of poetry, including *What Keeps Us Here* and *Soul Train*. *What Keeps Us Here* was the winner of Ampersand Press' 1992 Women Poets Series Competition. It also received the John C. Zacharis First Book Award from *Ploughshares* and Emerson College in Boston. Currently she is an Associate Professor at Southern Illinois University, Carbondale, where she serves as editor for *Crab Orchard Review* and director of the Young Writers Workshop, a summer conference for high school-aged writers. Her sixth collection, *My Father's Kites*, will be published by Steel Toe Books.

Joseph writes: "I wrote "Xenophilia" as an antidote to all the xenophobia present in American culture. Unless we are Native Americans, we all came to the United States from somewhere else. I wrote the poem so that I could wrap my arms around the Old World as well as the New World. I was thinking of immigration, of old customs, of steamer trunks of old clothes. In writing the poem, I was particularly thinking of the strength of women — thus the references to lace, etc. I wanted this poem to be a comfort to its readers, a way of remembering and embracing what should be enduring. I hope, that in some small way, it provides to readers a bit of the solace I felt when writing it."

Fady Joudah is a Palestinian-American poet and physician. He is the winner of the Yale Series of Younger Poets Competition for his collection of poems *The Earth in the Attic*. Joudah was born in Austin, Texas in 1971 to Palestinian refugee parents, and grew up in Libya and Saudi Arabia. He returned to the United States to study to become a doctor, first attending the University of Georgia in Athens, and then the Medical College of Georgia, before completing his medical training at the University of Texas. Joudah currently practices as an ER physician in Houston, Texas. He has also volunteered abroad with the humanitarian organization Doctors Without Borders.

Ilya Kaminsky was born in Odessa, former Soviet Union in 1977. In 1993, his family received asylum from the American government and came to the United States. Ilya received his BA from Georgetown University and subsequently became the youngest person ever to serve as George Bennet Fellow Writer in Residence at Phillips Exeter Academy. *Dancing in Odessa* is his first full length book.

Sophia Kartsonis is the writer of *Intaglio*, a collection of poems. She is an assistant professor at Columbus College of Art and Design.

Kartsonis writes: "'Cisterna' happened because I was interested in bending the sestina and the ear with both the form of opening with one-word lines in the first stanza and too, having those words carry the inevitability of the teleutons. I liked the play off sounds: cistern, sister, sestina and the way a word like say, "well" can suggest both underground water and well-being. I didn't begin with any kind of philosophical or political agenda but the words suggested their own and the buoyancy of both form and language allowed a tone more whimsical than didactic. But I saw also, just how it is that words mean, even when we try to entertain ourselves with their shapes and sounds, that cargo of meaning and cargo of what-matters often finds them. My interest in the women of my family, of my culture and their gleaming-knowledge, even as they were unable to resist the consequences of being born women at a moment and in a culture with additional challenges that made it hard to cry out loudly enough to save them, I think that all of that comes through. Theirs is a well-deep wisdom to them and I hope that something in the poem calls to that. This poem is one of those that upon finishing it, the writer decides that the fun in writing it might have to be enough as the poem may not resonate for others. I have been surprised at how often people sight this one and happy for those well-wishers — each and every."

Laura Kasischke is the author of thirteen books of poetry and fiction. Her novel *Her Life Before Her Eyes* was adapted for the screen and starred Uma Thurman. A Guggenheim Fellow in 2009, she teaches in the MFA program at the University of Michigan.

Susanna Lang's collection of poems, *Even Now*, was published by The Backwaters Press. More recently, her poem "Condemned" won the Inkwell competition, judged by Major Jackson. A poem published in *The Spoon River Poetry Review* won a 1999 Illinois Arts Council award. She lives with her family in Chicago, and works as a curriculum coach for the Chicago Public Schools.

Lang writes: "I wrote "Out the Window" a year ago, after reading an article in the New York Times that recounted how young people in the capital of Moldova, convinced that the Parliamentary election had been stolen from them, had used Twitter and other social media to bring crowds into the street, much as the Iranians would do over the summer ("After a 'Spontaneous' Riot, Moldovans Look for Answers," by Ellen Barry, April 9, 2009). I copied the phrase, "office papers tangled in the boughs of pine trees," into my notebook, and the image continued to haunt me. More than two weeks later, I wrote a first draft of the poem, which already started with the view out the kitchen window. For me, this poem crystallized a way to think about the poetry of witness which I had been struggling to write for years, while I worried about whether I had a right to the stories of others, and whether I could interest an audience in lives so far removed from their own. My writing group, which has been meeting monthly for the last 17 years, was doubtful, but I felt like these were the poems I needed to write. "Out the Window" gave me a way to make the stories my own: I understood that I need to create a "hinge" between my world and the world I am trying to enter through the poems, so that each poem connects my voice and the voices of those whose struggles I want to honor. In this case, the kitchen window led me to the windows overlooking the square where office papers decorated the trees and bore witness to the fierce desires of those who live on the other side of the world, but not so far removed from our own fierce desires."

Shirley Geok-lin Lim is a Professor in the English Department at the University of California, Santa Barbara. Her books include five books of poems; three books of short stories; two books of criticism; a book of memoirs, *Among the White Moon Faces: An Asian-American Memoir of Homelands*, and a novel, *Joss and Gold*.

Sonja Livingston's work has been honored with a NYFA Fellowship, Iowa Review Award, AWP Intro Award, and Pushcart Prize nominations. A memoir, *Ghostbread*, won the AWP Book Award, and is available from the University of Georgia Press.

Livingston writes: "My in-laws are the best people I know. They stand on corners with signs, write letters to editors and congressional representatives, send medical supplies to Cuba, organize potlucks, community projects, publish news-letters, resettle refugees, and so on. I love them. I love that they do these things with open hearts, and see the way they change lives. And I occasionally still hold a sign and sing on street corners, protesting war or calling for marriage equality. This poem, however, comes from an early experience of activism; sitting-in to protest American aggression in the Gulf, and what it was like for me. I did hate the idea of war, and liked feeling like a renegade, and it was exciting to be part of an important cause, but I've never felt good about lying to the secretary in D'Amato's office. Some say the ends justify the means and maybe they do; most likely they do. But that sit-in was too much like the invasion we were protesting, and for me, it was a moment of realization that the real war (or peace) I wage lies in the basics of everyday interaction in my community."

Clay Matthews's first book, *Superfecta*, is available from Ghost Road Press, and his second, *Runoff*, was recently released from BlazeVOX Books.

Matthews writes: "I'm always surprised how much I get to learn as a teacher. Sure, there's the regular grind and belly-aching, but, every semester, I have access to all these individuals and all of this new information. Sometimes that informa-tion is humorous. Sometimes shocking. Sometimes it really breaks my heart, too, as was the case with Matthew. Working with him on his essay about all of the horri-ble things that had happened to him and his family really made me realize how much of a bubble I live in. I can read about this stuff, see it all over the news, empa-thize, and get sad, but there's something about hearing a story from someone who really experienced it, seeing the story happen all over again in their eyes and ges-tures, that is unequivocally one of the most moving things in the world to me."

Richard Michelson is a poet and children's book author. *Battles & Lullabies* was selected by ForeWord as one of the 12 best poetry books of 2006. Michelson's books for children have received many honors. He has been a finalist for both the Massachusetts Book Award and the National Jewish Book Award. He has twice been the recipient of a Skipping Stones Multicultural Book Award. *As Good As Anybody: Martin Luther King and Abraham Joshua Heschel's Amazing March Toward Freedom* was awarded the Sydney Taylor Gold Medal from the "Association of Jewish Librarians." His latest picture book, *Busing Brewster*, is about forced school busing in the 1970's.

Michelson writes: "When I was born in 1953, my area of East New York, Brooklyn, was 90-percent Jewish. A short 12 years later, less than 10 percent of those living in the neighborhood were Jews. My dad had a hardware store and among my occasional duties was chaining up the garbage cans he had lined up for sale outside the store, so that "the shvartzers couldn't steal them." This poem came about when I was recalling a NYC garbage strike. I had neglected to bolt the lock and two cans were soon missing, but the trash was still piled high on the sidewalk.

I grew up confused about race. The great majority of my father's customers were polite, churchgoing Negroes. My Dad loved to joke with his regulars. In the days before political correctness, this often consisted of ethnic jokes. He made fun of their people and they made fun of his people. Then everyone laughed. I grew up comfortable with racial stereotyping, yet thinking blacks and Jews were best friends with a common economic enemy.

But by the time my Dad was shot on Pitkin Avenue during a robbery attempt, times had changed.

Had I been there, I might have tried to explain how Jews were instrumental in the founding of the NAACP and fighting civil liberty abuses during the 1960's. Had I been there, I might have mentioned that the Jewish flight wasn't just a natural evolution toward suburbs. The establishment always pits the outsider against the outsider, and there was an orchestrated attempt by those with power to benefit financially. Bankers saw a chance to get rich quick if they could scare the Jews into leaving en masse, and buy the abandoned buildings at rock bottom prices. Young blacks were paid to walk through the neighborhood and start fights. High rents were charged to the blacks (and later Hispanics) that moved in. Capitalizing on "fear of the other" is the one subject speculators quickly master. But now I am writing an essay, and what I wrote was a poem."

Derek Mong is the author of *Other Romes*. He and his wife, the translator Anne O. Fisher, are currently at work on the selected poetry of Maxim Amelin (Russian, b. 1970), tentatively titled *The Joyous Science*.

Mong writes: "From the fall of 2006 to the spring of 2007, I spent a lot of time on small, commuter planes, traveling between Madison, Wisconsin — where I was the Halls Poetry Fellow at UW — and Cleveland, Ohio — the nearest city to the college where my future wife taught. Inevitably, and at least once per flight, I'd imagine the plane dropping into freefall. This was, I suppose, a reaction to the still new security measures, the colorized threat levels, and the war. As the daydream reoccurred, I began to shape it, till the scenario became a grotesque, if comforting, ballet. I would later ask myself just what it meant to enter and share (in the form of a poem) that imaginative space. My college roommate had one answer. He mailed me, after reading the poem, a ream of stationary he'd somehow managed to procure from the Department of Homeland Security."

Idra Novey is the author of the poetry collection *The Next Country*. She has received fellowships from the National Endowment for the Arts, the Poetry Society of America, and the PEN Translation Fund. Her recent translations include the selected poems of Brazilian writer Manoel de Barros and a novel by Emilio Lascano Tegui, *On Elegance While Sleeping*. She currently directs the Center for Literary Translation at Columbia University and teaches at Columbia and NYU.

Novey writes: "For three years, I taught composition and poetry in a women's prison as part of a Bard College program that offers incarcerated men and women the chance to obtain a college degree. On the weekends, I would often think about my students inside the prison while I was out riding my bike or reading a book in the park or sitting down for dinner with my family. My first year teaching at the prison was also the first year Bard College offered classes there and it was an intense, anxious time. After every class, the students would stay with questions about the reading and about where they might transfer to finish their degrees when they were released. Getting to know that first group of students so closely, talking with them about the crimes they'd committed, and mourning together each time someone else in the class was denied parole, led me to think further about what prison and punishment have come to mean in this country, and for whom."

Naomi Shihab Nye was born to a Palestinian father and an American mother. During her high school years, she lived in Ramallah in Jordan, the Old City in Jerusalem, and San Antonio, Texas, where she later received her B.A. in English and world religions from Trinity University. She is the author of numerous books of poems, including *You and Yours* and *19 Varieties of Gazelle: Poems of the Middle East*, a collection of new and selected poems.

Hilton Obenzinger writes poetry, fiction, criticism and history. His most recent book is the autobiographical novel *Busy Dying*. He teaches writing and American studies at Stanford.

Obenzinger writes: "Occupy Wall Street is filled with the exuberance and joy of people all over the country spontaneously, autonomously taking action, redefining everything and creating a new language in the process — Occupy as noun and verb and adjective, but also as a state of mind, filling public space with masses of people who insist on being heard. Most of the encampments are gone by this time, but the movement against corporate greed, injustice and war is far from over. All those folks in New York and Oakland and Madrid and Cairo brought me this poem — and now you can write one too. Occupy your own words."

Julie Sophia Paegle is worried about how to, in the words of Betty Boop, "Be Human" on the planet right now. She teaches in the graduate program at CSU San Bernardino and lives in the San Bernardino Mountains with her husband and sons. Her poetry collection is *torch song tango choir*, which explores her dual Argentine and Latvian heritage.

Paegle writes: "When the Nazis and Soviets divided up Europe in the Molotov-Ribbentrop pact, Latvia fell on the border separating the Nazi from the Soviet spheres. Hitler broke this pact in 1941 and invaded and occupied Latvia until the war's end in 1944. More than 200,000 Latvians died during this period. Having expelled the Nazis in 1944, the Russians reoccupied Latvia until after Latvian independence and did not withdraw all its troops until 1994. The sequence of protests and rallies held by Estonians, Latvians, and Lithuanians beginning in 1988 contributed significantly to the Latvian independence won in 1991. These rallies were collectively called the Singing Revolution for the prominent role of folk songs suppressed under the Soviets.

These folk songs have since gained global recognition thanks to the Latvian

Boys' Choir, which toured the world after independence. I first heard the choir perform in Salt Lake City in 2000, just after I accompanied my Latvian born father on his first return trip to Latvia since his family fled in 1944. After my paternal grandfather joined the Latvian Resistance, my grandmother walked from Latvia to Germany, carrying with her my two-year old father and his new-born sister. The family spent five years in Displaced Persons camps throughout Germany until 1950, when they immigrated to California, thanks to sponsorship from the First Presbyterian Church of Hollywood. While we think my father's father starved during the war, we are still not certain of his fate; our first and subsequent returns to Latvia have turned up nothing conclusive.

I'll never forget the boys' beatific singing, and how their voices opened the low ceiling of their Temple Square performance space, as if to the loft and arc of the Riga Dome, or of the sky."

Anne Panning is the author of *The Price of Eggs* and *Super America*. Originally from Minnesota, Anne has lived in The Philippines, Vietnam, Hawaii, northern Idaho and Ohio; she now lives in upstate New York with her husband and two children, and teaches creative writing at SUNY-Brockport.

Panning writes: "I've always preferred to keep my politics private — to an extent. I say no to election signs in my front yard; I don't splatter my car with bumper stickers. I did, however, go stand outside on our front stoop the night Barrack Obama was elected and hoot and holler until my voice was raw (I was a little drunk). Anyway, having two small children has complicated my political self over time. For years I'd been meaning to attend our town's Take Back the Night march, but had found myriads of excuses not to. But as my kids grew older, I thought that my son, Hudson, should know about this. He should experience what equal rights really mean. I bribed him with promises of soda and pop; he was handed a sign which he wasn't very excited to carry (and I don't think he had any clue what it meant). It was a freezing cold night, and my husband and daughter were happily at home watching, "America's Funniest Videos" on the warm cozy couch (our daughter was too little to go). I marched, chanted, felt alternately moved to tears by the solidarity of all these women yet frustrated by the lack of men/boys. Hudson did everything he could to make sure I knew how miserable he was: dragging his feet, slumping his shoulders, complaining about the weather, pulling on my arm. I was a feminist; my husband was a feminist; I wanted my son to be a feminist. But was it really necessary to impose my politics and my feminism on my eight year old son? Hudson had always been more "feminine" than "masculine" in his traits and preferences. He was sensitive and preferred cuddling to sports. Someday I hope to show him this poem when I find out what kind of man he has become."

D.A. Powell was born in Albany, Georgia. He has won the Lyric Poetry Award from the Poetry Society of America, a grant for the National Endowment for the Arts, and a Paul Engle Fellowship. His second collection, *Lunch*, was a finalist for the National Poetry Series, and his third book, *Cocktails*, was a finalist for the National Book Critics Circle Award for Poetry. After the publication of *Chronic* in 2009, Claremont Graduate University announced that Powell had won its prestigious Kingsley Tufts Poetry Award.

Minnie Bruce Pratt is a lesbian writer and white anti-racist, anti-imperialist activist, born in 1946, in Selma, Alabama. She took her Ph.D. in English Literature at the University of North Carolina at Chapel Hill. In addition to this academic education, she received her education into the great liberation struggles of the 20th century through grass-roots organizing with women in the army-base town of Fayetteville, North Carolina, and through teaching at historically Black universities. Her essay, "Identity: Skin Blood Heart," now considered a feminist classic, chronicles some of this organizing and is used in universities nationally and internationally. Her poetry as a lesbian mother, was chosen for the Lamont Poetry Selection of the Academy of American Poets. Other honors include the American Library Association Gay and Lesbian Book Award for Literature, the Lambda Literary Award, and the Lillian Hellman — Dashiell Hammett Award from the Fund for Free Expression. She does organizing with the International Action Center and its Women's Fightback Network, and teaches at Syracuse University.

Pratt writes: "'Passing the Food Up and Down the Table' is from a series of poems I began to write after the U.S. invaded Afghanistan in 2001. Over many years in political work, I have thoroughly understood that capitalism, as a system, is unjust and oppressive, and leads over and over to terrible wars of aggression by the U.S. and terrible repression within the U.S. Yet this system seems to be accepted as "inevitable," even "natural," by every mainstream public voice around me — by the media, school systems, religious institutions, literary establishment, government officials. This reminds me dreadfully of how, when I was growing up in Alabama, every public authority (who were all white people) said that apartheid-like segregation was "God-given" and "good." But a political movement of people, led by African-American grass-roots organizers, overturned that brutally unjust system through fierce struggle. That taught me that there are always people seeing, feeling, thinking, and working against injustice in ways not allowed to be seen or heard at the public level. Now, as a poet under capitalism, I want to make that hidden, resistant life under an oppressive system visible and audible. So I walk around where I live and work, listening to "ordinary, working people." These are the people who are trying to survive, disrupt, counter, even overthrow and replace capitalism. Their realities and words are in the poems collected into "Inside the Money Machine with Nothing to Lose" (Carolina Wren, 2011). This particular poem took place in the West Village, New York City, after a conference convened by Workers World Party, when a crowd of us went out to eat together afterwards, and an organizer from Baltimore talked about her life as we "passed food up and down the table."

Robert Pringle is the author of *Cold Front* and a consultant to The Muse Machine, Dayton, Ohio. He was a metal worker and takes pride in his Scottish heritage.

Of "A Station in Ohio," Pringle writes: "I grew up in a house built some time before 1857, which has a basement as partially described in the poem. In cleaning, we found a wood-frame slate tablet with the previous owner's name, Bartels, and that date. Local history has the house as a stop on the underground railroad. I wanted to use that time since it connected with the Dred Scott decision."

Of "A 1969 Version of 'Soon,'" Pringle writes: "Ronnie was one of the foster children my wife, Patricia, and I had from 1968 until 1984. He walked early, was game for most any adventure, and was tough — bumps, bruises, rough-housing with other kids — he came up smiling, rarely a tear. He was the antithesis of the racist attitudes we found on our trip."

Judy Ray was the first executive director of The Writers Place in Kansas City. Her recent chapbooks are *Fishing in Green Waters* and *Sleeping in the Larder: Poems of a Sussex Childhood*. In Tucson she spends some of her time as a volunteer teacher of English as a Second Language to adults in the community.

Gabriela Erandi Rico is A P'urhepecha Indian poet and scholar. She was born in Michoacán, Mexico and grew up along the American west-coast following the migrant farm-worker trail. After graduating from Stanford, she toured the country as a spoken word performance poet with INCITE's Sisterfire! Cultural Arts Tour for Radical Women of Color. Gabriela's poetry has been published in various anthologies including: *We Got Issues! A Young Woman's Guide to Living a Bold, Courageous and Empowered Life, Ahani: Indigenous American Poetry, Mujeres de Maiz, Mujeres Poetas en el Pais de las Nubes*, and Rosa Linda Fregoso's forthcoming anthology, *Gender Terrorism: Feminicides in the Américas*. In 2008, she was the recipient of the Xochiquetzalli Award for Native American Women's Poetry. She's currently working on a poetry manuscript titled *Sunrise Ceremony for an Illegitimate Daughter*, and a novella tentatively called *Yanella*, about a girl of mixed Chicana/Dakota background who is kidnapped and trafficked into Tijuaja at the age of 14. As a Ph.D. candidate in Ethnic Studies at U.C. Berkeley, Gabriela teaches Chicana/o Studies program and Comparative Ethnic Studies. Her research focuses on contemporary issues affecting indigenous communities in Mexico; including recently-completed fieldwork on mestiza/o/Mexican consumption of P'urhepecha cultural and spiritual performances in her native Michoacán.

Rico writes: "This piece addresses the different forms of violence and displacement that Native/Indigenous peoples have endured in the Americas since the arrival of Christopher Columbus upon our continent. From the holocaust and dispossession of native peoples during the Spanish "Conquest" to the forced removal of tribes by the American government for the purposes of Western expansion in the 19th Century, indigenous peoples have endured 518 years of genocide, cultural eradication, and displacement. Today's forms of neo-colonial violence include the exploitation of our natural resources, the appropriation of our spirituality, high rates of social ills and diseases introduced by European colonialism (including diabetes, alcoholism, suicide, and drug-abuse on indigenous communities and reservations), and neo-liberal trade policies such as the FTAA and NAFTA, which displace our traditional lifeways and force our people to migrate in search of survival in a globalized world. All the while, we sing and dance our traditions, and we endure and survive....as this poem does."

Lois Roma-Deeley is the author of three collections of poetry, most recently *High Notes*. She has won numerous awards and honors for her poetry, including awards for the Allen Ginsberg Poetry Competition and the Emily Dickinson Poetry Competition, and recognition as a finalist in the Paumanok International Poetry Contest. She has published in ten national anthologies, including *New Hungers for Old: One-Hundred Years of Italian-American Poetry* as well as *The American Voice in Poetry: the Legacy of Whitman, Williams, and Ginsberg*, American Book Award winner *Looking For Home and Letters to the World* and others. In addition, Roma-Deeley was nominated for Arizona Governor's Arts Awards and the Pushcart award. She has been a finalist for the Emerging Writers fellowship.

Roma-Deeley writes: "The title is a bible reference found in the first book of Kings 19: 11 -12 (King James Version). This is when the prophet Elijah, weary and despairing, goes to the mountain to find God. There is a wind, then an earthquake. But that is not the Lord. Finally, he hears "a still small voice" and that is God. Similarly, in order for social justice to be realized in society, a person must resist the "whirlwinds and earthquakes" created by those who use fear to distort and deform the truth. Fear of change comes in many forms and guises, often accompanied by the idea that the consequences of change bring about great disaster: politically, religiously, and culturally. So, like Elijah, we must learn to listen, first, to our own deepest sense of rightness even when it does not match our initial expectations or the strident messages of the larger culture. Using that sense, we can fight demagogues such as Fr. Charles Coughlin, who used the radio to spread anti-semitism in the 1930s; Sen. Joseph McCarthy, who in the 1950s preyed on fears of communism to ruin the lives of anyone who disagreed with him; and various politicians in the 1960s who kept race hatred alive by retaining "Jim Crow" laws which, among many consequences, made segregation legal and customary."

Margaret Rozga is the author of two books. *Two Hundred Nights and One Day* tells the story of the Milwaukee NAACP Youth Council's successful campaign including 200 consecutive nights of marching for fair housing legislation. This book was awarded a bronze medal in poetry in the 2009 Independent Publishers Book Awards and named an outstanding achievement in poetry for 2009 by the Wisconsin Library Association. Rozga's play about the Milwaukee fair housing marches, *March On Milwaukee*, has seen three full productions and four concert readings since its debut at UW Waukesha in 2007. Her new book, *Though I Haven't Been to Baghdad*, presents poems written in response to the deployment of her Army Reservist son first to Iraq and later to Afghanistan.

Rozga writes: "What I love most about people who have been involved in movements for social justice is their creativity, and the response to police harassment chronicled in "Where Lawrence Learns the Law" provides an example of responding creatively to those in power and authority who would use their power to intimidate. I remember this event clearly. I grew up and was living less than a mile from Milwaukee Police Chief Harold Breier. The young men of the Milwaukee NAACP Youth Council who guarded the chief of police without a private detective's license used my car for this action. One morning about a week later, I found all four tires of my car had been slashed during the night as it was parked outside behind my home. My good parents calmly filed an insurance claim and bought new tires for my car, never saying a word to discourage my involvement in the civil rights movement."

Jason Schneiderman is the author of *Sublimination Point* and *Striking Surface*. He has received fellowships from Yaddo, The Fine Arts Work Center, and The Bread Loaf Writers' Conference. He has been the recipient of the Emily Dickinson Award from the Poetry Society of America in 2004.

Schneiderman writes: "My first experience of a national tragedy was when the Challenger exploded. Much of the news coverage was about how traumatized schoolchildren were by the explosion, which struck me as bizarre, since as a schoolchild, I didn't feel the least bit traumatized. In fact, my response, and the response of every other kid I knew was actually quite callous. We weren't telling Christa McCauliffe jokes because we were covering our pain; we were telling Christa McCauliffe jokes because we thought they were funny. I felt a huge disconnect between my experience and the national discourse, but I had no way to talk back. Now I can talk back. This is what I wanted to say."

Tim Seibles is the author of five collections of poetry, most recently, *Buffalo Head Solos*. He is a professor of English and creative writing at Old Dominion University, as well as teaching in the Stonecoast MFA Program in Creative Writing and teaching workshops for Cave Canem.

Don Share is Senior Editor of *Poetry* magazine in Chicago. His books include *Squandermania*, *Union*, *The Traumatophile*, and *Seneca in English*; forthcoming are *Bunting's Persia*, and a critical edition of Basil Bunting's poems. His translations of Miguel Hernández, collected in *I Have Lots of Heart* were awarded the Times Literary Supplement Translation Prize, the Premio Valle Inclán Prize, and the PEN/New England Discovery Award. He has been Poetry Editor of *Harvard Review* and *Partisan Review*, Editor of *Literary Imagination*, and Curator of Poetry at Harvard University.

Share writes: "At the time I was writing the poem – which was not long after 9/11 — I was fortunate enough to be working just steps away from a darkened room full of Emily Dickinson's personal belongings in the Houghton Library at Harvard: her piano, her books, her jewelry, writing table, even a sampler she made as a child. I feel that Dickinson's poems were meant to be very moral – not as in judgmental (though she is judgmental) or in terms of telling someone what to do, but rather as indicating the paths a lost or obscure person could navigate to something resembling a good place. I needed that then, and in a dream-like state, she transmitted the words "cryptonyms" and "influentials" to me. They are mysterious, as poem-words always were, and stern. My poem is explicitly angry. The first and last stanzas aren't obscure. They demand social justice. The lines in-between them are about longing, avidity, vertigo. I did not know, but needed to know, how to conduct my life."

Glenn Sheldon is a poet and a professor of English at The University of Toledo. He is the author of a critical monograph, as well as two full-length poetry books: *Bird Scarer* and *Angel of Anarchy*. The first half of his professional life was spent, generally, as an editor of political journalism; he has been teaching at the University of Toledo now for over a dozen years.

Sheldon writes: "I was reading Thomas McGrath's *Selected Poems* (I've done a lot of critical work on him), when I found this phrase from a scribbled sidebar comment I had written on one of his poems. I knew it had to be the title ('Years Unite to Become Centuries') for a poem, though I don't think it's the most poetic phrasing in the world (on an aesthetic level). The phrasing just suddenly struck me: the amount of violence around the world I'd been "exposed to" via the media since adulthood, or since I was aware of the greater world in which I dwell. I had this rush of a sense of accumulation in just the decades I'd lived through. Then I thought about all I had been taught, all the history, all the wars (not just military conflicts but cultural ones, as well). And I thought I needed to write a poem about how time erodes the pain of suffering, as well as about how time must also serve as a reminder of past errors in judgment that can lead us to better judgments that may, hopefully, lead us into a more peaceful world. McGrath has this concept of the "fifth season," which is a metaphor for hope; he utilizes the Blue Star Kachina as the harbinger of that change. And I had to reflect on what my own metaphors were for hope, and at least here, I think it's words and word-workers and books and libraries. Knowledge. I believe in the power of words to change the world, even if only in small ways sometimes. But full-scale revolutions are also built on words. Genocide, too, can be built upon words. Thus I wanted the revelatory here, as well as the celebratory: kisses, laughter, toasts, a stampede of hopeful change in the face of often grim global realities."

Peggy Shumaker's most recent book is the memoir *Just Breathe Normally*. As a writer in residence for the Arizona Commission on the Arts, Peggy worked with prison inmates, honors students, gang members, deaf adults, teen parents, little kids, library patrons, and elderly folks.

Patricia Smith is the author of five books of poetry, including *Blood Dazzler*, chronicling the tragedy of Hurricane Katrina, a finalist for the 2008 National

Book Award. She also authored the ground-breaking history *Africans in America* and the award-winning children's book *Janna and the Kings*. She has performed around the world, including Carnegie Hall, the Poets Stage in Stockholm, Rotterdam's Poetry International, the Aran Islands International Poetry and Prose Festival, the Bahia Festival, the Schomburg Center and on tour in Germany, Austria and Holland. She is a Pushcart Prize winner and a four-time individual champion of the National Poetry Slam, the most successful poet in the competition's history. A professor at the City University of New York/College of Staten Island, she also serves on the faculty of both Cave Canem and the Stonecoast MFA program at the University of Southern Maine.

Of "And Now, The News: Tonight the Soldiers," Smith writes: "When I was a kid, the Vietnam War horrified me. The images on television were brutal, unfiltered and, for the most part, unexplained. Neither of my parents, busy forging an existence in the brick cornfields of Chicago, thought it necessary to help me make sense of the chaos, so I was left alone to witness and decipher the screams, the smoke, the blood. Keep in mind, this was in the staid era of Mary Tyler Moore and Dick Van Dyke playing a married couple but cooing at each other from separate beds. The country lost its damned mind when black entertainer Nat King Cole pecked one of his white female guests on the cheek in greeting. Donna Reed and her stiff-coifed crew represented the best there was in American family. In the midst of all this determined whitewashing, there was this war, this very public bloodletting.

To keep myself from going crazy, I imagined the soldiers in a bit of unraveling dramatic entertainment, a snippet of wildly realistic cinema. I couldn't stop looking, so I had to convince myself that I was seeing something other than what I was. In my dreams, the soldiers paused in the midst of the madness, turned to wink at me from the television screen, and began to dance — slowly at first, then feverishly. The blood still stained their uniforms, their skulls were still blown open, legs were interrupted at the knee. But I forced them to dance. I dressed an ugly and insistent reality up in a funny little hat.

The Vietnam War is over. The soldiers are younger. The backdrop has changed. I still need the dream."

Of "Rebuilding," Smith writes: "Writing the book about Katrina was incredibly difficult. As anyone who is a poet knows, pulling together any manuscript is a tricky undertaking — you have to balance the long poems, the short poems, the funny poems, the serious poems, the structured poems, the free-verse offerings, the moody pieces, the frivolous and political poems. With Katrina, there was really only one way to enter and leave most of the poems, and that path was a tragic one. Although some perspectives were funny in an infuriating way (say hello to George Bush and his friend Michael Brown), every word I wrote sounded a blue note."

I wanted to include at least one poem that hinted at resurrection. "Rebuilding" is that poem."

Nicole Walker is the author of *This Noisy Egg*. She has received a fellowship from the National Endowment for the Arts. She is currently an Assistant Professor at Northern Arizona University.

Walker writes: "While driving through the Navajo Reservation, I feel like I'm trespassing. It's a beautiful, if dry and desolate landscape, marked by ruins, both manmade and geologic. Great red canyon walls are backdrops for stone buildings, trailers, gas stations. There are dogs there. Skinny dogs with no tags. These dogs don't have owners in the traditional sense but they are the dogs of the reservation. The land and the people collectively watch over them. It's a kind of ownership I'll never understand and thinking that I can take care of the dog better is the same sort of hubris that suggested that white people could take better care of New York, Nebraska, Oklahoma or Arizona. The Native Americans have been taking care in bigger ways than I can understand. The best way I can help is to get out of their way."

Afaa Michael Weaver is Alumnae Professor of English at Simmons College in Boston. He is the author of nine previous books of poetry including *The Plum Flower Dance*, *My Father's Geography* and *Timber and Prayer* as well as short fiction and plays. He has been named a Pew Fellow in Poetry and the first Elder of Cave Canem, and was the first African American poet to hold the poet-in-residence position at the Stadler Poetry Center at Bucknell University.

Estha Weiner is co-editor and contributor to *Blues For Bill: A Tribute To William Matthews*, and author of *The Mistress Manuscript*, and *Transfiguration Begins At Home*.

Jillian Weise calls herself a cyborg. She is also the author of *The Amputee's Guide to Sex* and *The Colony*.

Patricia Jabbeh Wesley's new book of poems, *Where the Road Turns*, was published by Autumn House Press.

Crystal Williams was raised in Detroit, MI and Madrid, Spain. She earned a B.A. at New York University and a Master of Fine Arts at Cornell University. She is currently Associate Professor at Reed College in Portland, OR and divides her time between Oregon and Chicago. She is the author of three poetry collections: *Troubled Tongues*, *Kin* and *Lunatic*.

Eliot Khalil Wilson's first collection of poems, *The Saint of Letting Small Fish Go*, won the 2003 Cleveland State Poetry Prize. He currently lives in Colorado.

Wilson writes: "I wanted to say something about what I consider to be the gross injustice of the 2000 mile Mexican border fence and the ignorant violence associated with the border patrols. The lessons of Berlin and the Cold War seem to be forgotten, but there is still, (as Frost would have it), something that doesn't love a wall, that wants it down. Sadly, the particulars of the narrative are culled from actual news sources."

Jake Adam York is the author of three books of poems — *Murder Ballads, A Murmuration of Starlings,* and *Persons Unknown.* He now teaches at the University of Colorado Denver, where he co-edits *Copper Nickel* with his colleagues and students.

York writes: "Growing up near Birmingham in the 70s and 80s, Civil Rights history was ever present, but usually indistinct, out of focus. My parents and grandparents had lived through the murders and marches, legal battles and race riots, but in the bedroom community of Gadsden, everything seemed muffled by blankets.

When I was in college, many fortieth anniversaries came around, and with them renewed interest in unsolved crimes and documentaries often more direct than would ever have been possible before. Spike Lee's Four Little Girls, for example, froze me with autopsy photos. History came into brutal focus, and I began to adopt the documentarian's techniques in my poetic work."

"Vigil," approaches a story that is usually offered as an aside or a footnote — the murder of Virgil Ware on the day of the 16th Street Baptist Church bombing. The deaths of Addie Mae Collins, Denise McNair, Carole Robertson, and Cynthia Wesley are difficult to imagine together, and they make further imagination impossible. Ware's death blurs in the bokeh beyond the focal length.

His killers must have assumed this would happen, that in the swell of the day, the crime and the victim would blur. They sought to erase him.

But much survives — the stories, of course, in familial channels. But also the physical creatures of our lives. So, the bike Virgil and his brother were riding that day, how it must remain. How the history — as well as the history we must write to live with history — is waiting there if we choose to pick it up, however common or painful it may be. We touch it to rise out of sleep. We must awaken, whatever we will see when we open our eyes."

Copyright Pages

Sherman Alexie, "The Museum of Tolerance" from *The Business of Fancydancing* (Hanging Loose Press, 1992). Copyright © 1992 by Hanging Loose Press. Reprinted with permission of Hanging Loose Press.

Indran J. Amirthanayagam, "After Battle." Copyright © 2009 by Indran J. Amirthanayagam. Printed with permission from author.

Rane Arroyo, "In Praise of Shirley Chisholm." Copyright © 2009 by Rane Arroyo. Printed with permission from author.

David Baker, "The Spring Ephemerals" from *Midwest Eclogue* (W.W. Norton, 2005). Copyright © 2005 by W.W. Norton. Reprinted with permission from author.

Marvin Bell, "The Dead Have Nothing to Lose by Telling the Truth" appeared in *The Iowa Review* (1998). Copyright © 1998 by *The Iowa Review*. Reprinted with permission from author.

Dan Bellm, "The weight" from *Practice* (Sixteen Rivers Press, 2008). Copyright © 2008 by Sixteen Rivers Press. Reprinted with permission from author.

Patrick Bizzaro, "Not on the Rez" appeared in *Passwords* (2008-2009). Copyright © 2009 by Paresia Press. Reprinted with permission from editor.

Ralph Black, "21st Century Lecture" appeared in *Massachusetts Review* (Fall 2007). Copyright © 2007 by Massachusetts Press. Printed with permission from author.

Lindsey Brown, "The Clothesline Project." Copyright © 2010 by Lindsey Brown. Printed with permission from author.

Claudia Carlson, "After Ice and Rain." Copyright © 2010 by Claudia Carlson. Printed with permission from author.

Sarah Cedeño, "Vitamin D and Frisbees." Copyright © 2010 by Sarah Cedeño. Printed with permission from author.

Kevin Clark, "Elizabeth at Seabrook" from *Self-Portrait with Expletives* (LSU Press, 2010). Copyright © 2010 by LSU Press. Reprinted with permission from author.

Allison Hedge Coke, "America, I Sing Back" appeared in *Medellin Poetry Festival Journal* (2005). Copyright © 2005 by *Medellin Poetry Festival Journal*. Reprinted with permission from author.

Martha Collins, "Birmingham" from *Blue Front* (Graywolf Press, 2006). Copyright © 2006 by Graywolf Press. Reprinted with permission from editor.

Sean Thomas Dougherty, "After the Election" from *Broken Hallelujahs* (BOA, 2007). Copyright © 2007 by BOA. Reprinted with permission from BOA.·

Denise Duhamel, "David Lemieux" from *Queen for a Day* (University of Pittsburgh Press, 2002). Copyright © 2002 by University of Pittsburgh Press. Reprinted with permission from editor.

Cheryl Dumesnil, "Hard Labor" from *In Praise of Falling* (University of Pittsburg Press, 2009). Copyright © 2009 by University of Pittsburgh Press. Reprinted with permission from University of Pittsburgh Press.

Martín Espada, "Litany at the Tomb of Frederick Douglass" appeared in *The Bloomsbury Review* (May–July 2009). Copyright © 2009 by *The Bloomsbury Review*. Reprinted with permission from author.

Acknowledgements

Our heartfelt thanks to you, Le Roy and Lesly Chappell, for trusting us with this project. Over the years, you've become part of our family.

Warm gratitude to Lois Roma-Deeley and Scott Hightower for bringing so many poets to us.

We are thankful to Rigoberto González, David Kirby, Barbara Hamby, for inspiring us with their anthologies.

As always, we are grateful to Claudia Carlson for her amazing talent.

And to all the poets—as well as many kind publishers—who so generously waived the permission fees: it's thanks to you that this book is in the world.

About Benu Press

Benu Press is a small, independent press committed to publishing poetry, fiction, and creative non-fiction. We believe in the transformative power of literature. To that end, we seek to publish inspiring and thought-provoking books about the practical dimensions of social justice and equity.

Published by Benu Press:

March on Milwaukee: A Memoir of the Open Housing Protests (script),
    Margaret Rozga
Language is Power, Stephanie Reid
Confederate Streets, Erin Tocknell
Though I Haven't Been to Baghdad, Margaret Rozga
Love Rise Up, edited by Steve Fellner and Phil E. Young
High Notes, Lois Roma-Deeley
Two Hundred Nights and One Day, Margaret Rozga
All Screwed Up, Steve Fellner

For more information: http://www.benupress.com

green press
INITIATIVE